CAN WE TALK TO GOD?

CAN WE TALK TO GOD?

Formerly titled:
The Ebell Lectures on Spiritual Science

Ernest Holmes

Health Communications, Inc.
Deerfield Beach, Florida

www.hci-online.com

Library of Congress Cataloging-in-Publication Data

Holmes, Ernest, 1887–1960.
   [Selections. 1999]
   Can we talk to God? / Ernest Holmes.
      p.   c.m.
   "Formerly titled: The Ebell lectures on spiritual science."
   ISBN : 1-55874-736-2 (trade paper)
   1. United Church of Religious Science—Doctrines. 2. Spiritual
life—United Church of Religious Science. 3. Prayer—United Church
of Religious Science. I. Title.

BF605.U53 H625   1999
299'.93—dc21   99-044304
                                                          CIP

Publisher: Health Communications, Inc.
                3201 S.W. 15th Street
                Deerfield Beach, FL 33442-8190

R-06-00

Cover design by Larissa Hise
Book inside design by Dawn Grove

CONTENTS

PUBLISHER'S NOTE

This book, first copyrighted by Ernest Holmes in 1934, was taken from lectures given at the Wilshire Ebell Theatre in Los Angeles. Speaking early in the twentieth century, Dr. Holmes followed conventions of that era, using generic masculine forms in referring to both men and women. This new edition has been edited to reflect an inclusive style.

FOREWORD

When the wheat has been separated from the chaff, when the bottom line has been reached, most yearning hearts still ask . . . *Can We Talk to God?* It is the ancient longing, the perennial search. With profound clarity and compassion, Dr. Ernest Holmes shares bold realizations in the pages you are about to turn: You have been endowed with the answer to that question all along . . . and a life-changing conversation is about to be realized.

Yes, there is a divine communication, and this book will show you how to fulfill your role in it with confidence and assurance. Though they are spiritually natural, the results will seem miraculous. A newspaper report demonstrates this in the experience of an elderly man who was poor in resources yet rich in spirit. The sidewalk in front of his humble home was crumbling and no longer safe; however, he had no apparent means to replace it. Avoiding despair and drawing upon his spiritual riches, this man held his private talk with God, boldly declaring that it was high time for an answer. Following this prayer, he had his grandchildren haul away the broken concrete, and he used some boards to build new forms for the walkway. Then he declared, "God, I've done my part!" About ten days later, a truck full of cement drove down his street and tried to turn at his corner. But the truck was going too fast and overturned. The workers had to offload the cement quickly before it hardened inside the truck. The elderly man simply stepped onto his porch, pointed to the forms and shouted, "You can put that cement in here. Thank you, God!"

This is the essence of Dr. Holmes's message: The divine Substance—God's unlimited Good—is already prepared. Anyone ready to receive can build "new forms"—new forms in mind and heart—through effective prayer, affirmative prayer. The principles involved, though ancient, are relevant to any modern issue, challenge or opportunity. Using them first saved my life then blessed it many times over. They can do the same for you.

Dr. Ernest Holmes has been described as one of the most influential of spiritual pioneers. A colleague, Dr. Norman Vincent Peale, said of Holmes, "I believe God was in this man, Ernest Holmes. He was in tune with the Infinite." A free thinker all his life, Holmes studied the sacred texts of both East and West, marrying the core truths of both into a philosophy he called the Science of Mind and Spirit. It has become a transforming way for the millions who have discovered and applied its teachings.

Can We Talk to God? dissolves superstition and confusion by revealing the spiritual and creative powers in every person. There are many gifts prepared for you herein: a way to commune with the Infinite, new prayer power and proven tools to create the life you have always deserved. Are you ready to receive them? Take this book home and read it again and again. Then start building new forms . . . design your new pathway with the deep assurance that, in perfect ways you may not be able to foresee, God will fulfill it!

Dr. Roger W. Teel

[EDITORS' NOTE: *Dr. Roger W. Teel is senior minister of Mile Hi Church of Religious Science in Denver, Colorado, a spiritual community with over ten thousand members. His ministry, which began in 1976, is about opening hearts, inspiring lives and embracing dreams. He is also a founder of the Association for Global New Thought.*]

I

Can We Talk to God?

Can We Talk to God?

Can we talk to God? We all know we can talk *at* God, but it is a different proposition to consider whether we can talk *to* God. I am considering the topic from the standpoint of communication. Unless we are conscious that we are talking to God and God is conscious that He is being talked to, we certainly cannot communicate with God. There can be no real communication without a reciprocity of ideas. Either we can talk to God or we cannot. If we cannot, we may as well realize it and no longer try, and if we can, we feel certain that a little conversation with the Deity would do us more good than much conversation with each other.

In the old order of thought, we talked at God. We felt as though our prayers ascended and hit the Divine ear, and if this were true, they must too often have hit this Divine ear with a discordant note.

In the new idea of life, we are thinking of God as a Universal Principle, Intelligence, and Power; as the essence and energy of being. We are thinking of God— or attempting to, at least—in universal terms, but it is impossible for the finite to grasp the meaning of the Infinite. The Infinite signifies that which is beyond human knowledge. We are thinking of God as a universal and infinite Being, as perfect law, the immutable law of cause and effect, and in doing this, discarding the ancient idea of a huge person in the nature of the Deity, we are undoubtedly losing something; we are losing the sense of personal contact with this invisible power, and we are liable to think of God only as law, or as an Infinite It. Now an Infinite It is a very adequate thing in certain respects, but in other respects it is very inadequate. We could not derive much comfort, pleasure or joy from talking to the principle of chemical affinity (yet we do derive a great benefit from learning that such a law exists). Neither can we hope to get much satisfaction from thinking of God only as an Infinite It.

We are intelligent; we think, know and understand, at least, something. Can we suppose that we are accidents? Can we believe that the works of William Shakespeare

are the result of an explosion in a type factory?

There must be, and there is, a Universal consciousness which directly responds to our thought and is in contact with it. Not only does the human heart long for such a possibility, but the human mind comprehends, understands, senses, feels and knows it. There are moments when the individual consciousness feels itself merged with the Universal, then it knows and no longer asks for explanations. The heart longs for, the mind comprehends and the intellect needs such a contact—the influx of divine ideas stimulating the will to divine purposefulness. It is fundamental to our belief that there is a Presence in the universe with which we may consciously communicate and which will consciously respond to such communication. We hold this as fundamental to any consistent philosophy or religion, not only because we long for and actually need it, but because such a Presence is an inevitable necessity.

How can we assume that, with our finite minds, or even the united intelligence of finite minds, we comprehend all there is? How can we assume that a finite mind constitutes the only intelligence in the universe, or that there is nothing beyond our present comprehension? How can we assume that we could *be*, unless Being itself is a fact? Could we recognize anything unless Being itself is a fact? Could we recognize anything unless that which recognizes existed before the thing which is

recognized? With what is it, then, that we recognize
unless it is with some intelligence within us that is in
unity with the great and final Intelligence, the Eternal
Being? We have not, cannot and never shall exhaust Its
totality. But we must assume that this final Being is conscious of us as part of Itself, and if this be true, it must
be true that we can communicate with It. But we realize
that we cannot communicate with a God external to our
own nature of being, for the simple reason that we cannot know anything beyond our own knowledge. In
other words, there is an Intelligence and a responsive
Presence in the universe. There is a God who knows,
cares, understands and responds, but only through our
own nature.

We must be careful, in the transition from the old to
the new, not to knock props from under us which perhaps we still need; not to rob people of their God unless
we can give them a better one, for that is the most
destructive thing in the world. I would rather see someone with a poor idea of Deity, than to see him or her
have no concept of Deity at all, because we must all
interpret God through our perception of the Divine
Being. In the transition, then, let us be careful that in
place of every false supposition which we once had, we
shall find a divine reality which is an eternal verity.
There was never any counterfeit made until after there
had been a proven reality, and the idea which has been

instinctive in the mind of humanity—the idea of our personal relationship to the Deity—is not there without a reason. It is a proclamation that the Deity indwells our own soul and that we are intuitively conscious of this Divine Fact.

That instinctive sense of the Divine Presence which is inherent in us all is there because it is true, and in the state of each person's intellectual capacity to perceive truth, it comes out, and to each of us becomes our God. It is forever proclaiming its own being. There is a Power and a Presence in the universe which responds to us so completely, so perfectly, that we shall be amazed when we realize *how* completely, and *how* perfectly, but it can only operate for us through us. Our communication with God must of necessity be, and always remain, an inner light; we communicate with the indwelling God.

I doubt not that there is a God beyond our finite comprehension, for the nature of God is to be universal, but it is the nature of humankind to be so constituted that we can know nothing outside the confines of our own knowledge; this is self-evident. Hence, the only God we can know is the God which we sense, and since this is an inner light, it is God in and through us. This is the only God we *can* know; this is the God who responds to us, and I sense that in every altruistic act, in every true charity which is love, in every expression of right emotion, that this is God-action through the

individual, a direct response. And it is logical to suppose
that since the nature of God is constructive, is goodness,
peace, purity and love, light and wisdom, that we truly
communicate with the divine only as we truly approach
the nature of reality through harmony, through receptivity, peace and joy. And I can see that as our mental
attitudes hinder the divine from flowing through us we
do not approach God consciously; therefore we do not
contact harmony subjectively, and hence we suffer
objectively. This is the immutable Law of Cause and
Effect.

There is something in us that longs for the sympa-
thetic understanding, the kindly response, the sense of a
presence which is warm, pulsating and colorful. We
must have it, and I sense that as we meet each other in
love and friendship, in the warmth of a handshake and
in good fellowship, it is God. What else could it be? The
hand that gives is the hand of God, and the eye that sees
is the eye of God. In each other, through each other, we
contact God, but God is more than this. If this were the
only God there is, then the artist would have painted a
picture and stepped into it, being completely lost in his or
her own work. Now, do we say that art is greater than the
artist or thought greater than the mind which conceived
it? The poem is not the poet, who has breathed into,
animated and created it, and it will stay, so long as his
or her consciousness exists, but he or she has not

stepped into it; some day he or she will write another and a better poem. Neither is God absorbed by law or creation.

I think that as we contact each other we are contacting a definite, direct manifestation of Deity; when we talk to each other, I think that God is talking to God; but I do not think that this is the only God there is. If it were, our finite knowledge would have exhausted the Infinite and there would be no God beyond our conversation.

We long for a conscious approach to the Infinite. It is as necessary to the nature and the intellect of humankind as food is to the well-being of our physical bodies, this Divine nourishment. What is true on one plane is true on all. Those of us who are seeking to understand the truth, and the breadth, width and depth of Science of Mind must realize that these things are possible. Of what ultimate value would a religion or philosophy be to the world which simply taught it a few laws of cause and effect, or how to heal a pain? This is good and wonderful, but unless it teaches how to live and how to be, unless it gives something which is a divine certainty of life and being, it is useless.

Prosperity is inevitable if a person's mind is right. Nothing can stop it. Healing is inevitable if a person is in harmony with life. There is nothing that can stop it. It is a law. We are to use consciously this law, but we can use it only to the degree in which our consciousness is unified with Truth. But we must not go searching after God. God is in you and in me. Therefore we each must penetrate more deeply into our own nature, and just so surely as we do, we will have a very marvelous experience. We will find a depth to ourself that we have never realized. It will be a sane, spiritual experience. We will sense a something within that we never dreamed of. We have read about it, but we never dreamed it was within us. This is where we meet God. And we are going to learn this: that we can talk to God just as consciously as we talk to people, and that if we expect it, believe it and feel it, we will receive just as direct a response. We will not receive an audible word because God's audible word is placed, in this creation, in the mouths of individuals. This is the only audible word God has on this plane.

God speaks every time a scientist discovers a new thing, every time an inventor invents a new thing—God speaks, and wherever truth is proclaimed, God is speaking. But the person who goes deeply into his or her own nature will find that God speaks in a language more subtle than the human language, without a tongue, in that universal language of spiritual emotion which is instinctive in human and in brute, and held in common by all civilization, by all creation, by all people who have lived—the universal language of emotion, sense, feeling, intuition, instinct. Sometimes we call it *conscience,* sometimes we call it a hunch, sometimes we call it a vision, a dream. It makes no difference what we call it. It is a direct revelation of Omniscience through us.

And so we learn to go deeply into ourselves and to speak as though there were a Presence there which knows; and we should take the time to unearth this hidden cause, to penetrate this inner chamber of consciousness which but few people realize exists. It is most worthwhile to talk to the Universal Spirit, when we talk in the right way. Do not talk *at* It; talk *to* It. Sense and feel that It is within you, that the approach to It is direct, through your own consciousness. That It is just as conscious of you as you are of It—since your consciousness of It must be, in the last analysis, and is, Its consciousness of Itself. Hence as we recognize It, It recognizes us. As we go out to meet It, It comes out to meet us. This is the meaning of the story of the Prodigal Son. Always we are met halfway. Always the Spirit corresponds to our belief in and receptivity to It. Hence there is a power within, to which each may come; a Presence which is Light; a Spirit which is guidance. This is fundamental to the understanding of the Science of Mind. There is a Spirit which knows. This is God. This Spirit which knows, knows us. It corresponds, It responds. It flows through us. Whatever intelligence we have is It, in us.

We differentiate between the Law and the Spirit; the Spirit directs and guides, the Law executes, and creation is the result. This is the Trinity—the Thing, the way it works and what it does. The constructive use of the law—always seeking to use it in the right way, for good only—is what is meant by the Spirit of Christ. The destructive use of the law—using it only for selfish, personal or conflicting aims—is what is meant by the spirit of Antichrist. However, there is nothing in either the Spirit or the Law of the universe which denies us the most complete use of it, provided we use it constructively. In other words, God wants us to have more than we have. The Spirit desires a complete expression of Itself. Hence, the more we enjoy, the more It is expressed.

Consider the Spirit as a warm, pulsating, reciprocal thing. It presses against us; It flows through us. It is our intelligence. It is a great universal urge and surge. It is a warm colorful thing. It is a beautiful thing. It cannot be put into words. You can only feel it. But consider the Law as a cold fact, nothing else. It has no motive of its own. It is just a power, a blind force, but it is an intelligent, an executing and immutable force. The law is the servant of the Spirit. Consider creation—whether it be the vast body of the Cosmos, or the suit of clothes, or the dress we have on—as some effect of intelligence operating through law and you have the whole proposition as clear as can be that there is a power in the universe which knows, a law which does, a creation which corresponds. Creation does not respond, it only corresponds. Now that is what we mean when we speak of Divine Principle. Divine Principle is not God any more than electricity is God. It is a law of God, just as electricity is a law of God. It is a mental law of cause and effect. When you impress your thought upon it, it is its nature to take that thought and execute it, exactly as you think it. If there is destruction in the thought, it must destroy. If there is good in the thought, it will execute goodness or healing. This is the principle governing *spiritual science,* and, unless such a principle were, spiritual science could not be. Know that there is something more than law; an intelligence to which we may come for inspiration, for guidance, for direction; a power responding to us, a Presence pressing against us, an animation flowing through us, a light within us.

This is the constitution of Being, the Eternal God, the Everlasting Spirit, the Father.

The Unity of Truth

Science of Mind and Spirit bears the same relation to religion that natural science bears to the laws of nature. It is a science of mental and spiritual phenomena, and, as such, it appeals to adherents of all religious beliefs, as well as to those who have no particular religious conviction; it appeals to all students of life.

We all look to the day when science and religion shall walk hand in hand through the visible to the invisible. A movement which endeavors to unify the great conclusions of human experience must be kept free from petty ideas, from personal ambitions and from any attempt to promote one person's opinion. Science knows nothing of opinion, but recognizes a government of law whose principles are universal. These laws, when complied with, respond alike to all. Religion becomes dogmatic and often superstitious when based on the lengthened shadow of any one personality. Philosophy intrigues us only to the extent that it sounds a universal note.

The religionist who believes in a faith once and forever delivered to the saints is lost to a greater vision. The philosopher whose petty conclusions obstruct a broader viewpoint is traveling in a vicious circle, and any scientist who refuses to accept intangible values has no adequate basis for the tangibility of the values which he has already discovered.

The ethics of Buddha, the morals of Confucius, the beatitudes of Jesus, together with the deductions of other great minds, constitute viewpoints of life which should not be overlooked. The mystical concepts of the ancient sages of China keep faith with the sayings of Eckhart or Underhill; the deep thoughts of ages past are reworded in Emerson's *Essays,* and wherever deep cries unto deep, deep answers deep.

Science is already deserting its old materialistic basis and indulging in philosophic viewpoints. All branches of knowledge are converging, and a fundamental unity is becoming more and more evident. Revelation must keep faith with reason, and religion with law, while intuition is ever spreading its wings for greater flights; science must justify faith in the invisible.

All of us seek some relationship to the Universal Mind, the Oversoul or the Eternal Spirit which we call God. That we are living in a spiritual universe which includes the material or physical universe has been a conclusion of the deepest thinkers of every age. That this spiritual universe must be one of pure intelligence and perfect life, dominated by love, by reason and by the power to create, seems an inevitable conclusion.

We all wish to feel that the power behind everything is good as well as creative, an eternal and changeless Intelligence in which we live, move and have our being. Intuitively we sense that each of us, in our native state, is some part or manifestation of this eternal Principle, and that the entire problem of limitation, evil, suffering and uncertainty is not God-ordained, but is the result of ignorance. It has been written that the Truth shall make us free, provided we know the Truth, and we note that the evolution of humankind's consciousness brings with it the acquisition of new powers and higher possibilities.

Nature seems to await our comprehension of her, and, since she is governed by immutable laws, the ignorance of which excuses no person from their effects, the bondages of humanity must be a result of our ignorance of the true nature of Reality. But some people will say: "If the power behind everything is good, why does it admit of even the possibility of evil and limitation?" The only answer to this question is that we are each individuals left alone to discover ourselves, creatures of volition, intelligence and will, fused into personality for the purpose of producing a real entity—an actual, conscious being.

The storehouse of nature may be filled with good, but this good is locked to the ignorant. The key to this door is held in the mind of intelligence, working in accordance with universal law. Through experience we learn what is really good and satisfying, what is truly worthwhile. As our intelligence increases and our capacity to understand the subtle laws of nature grows, we will gradually be set free. As we learn the Truth, the Truth will automatically emancipate us.

The advancement of science, philosophy and religion is not the result of a change in the nature of Reality but of a change in our minds toward Reality. Reality, of course, is changeless and eternal. Is it possible that this ultimate Reality can hold less than liberty under law? This position may seem rather an idealistic one at first; perhaps rather an unreasonable one in the light of previous experiences; it seems too good to be true, and the experience of the race appears to contradict the assumption of an inherent freedom. But can we thus limit the Universe, that intelligent and creative law which, acting in accord with its own nature, subtly molds the invisible essence of its own being into the forms of creation? The Infinite is indeed Infinite even though the finite seems indeed finite. Who can set a limit even to that which we call finite? Have not all acquisitions of nature been a result of the discovery of truths and of latent laws and capacities unknown until they were discovered? If we have made such discoveries of physical and material laws, should it seem strange that we might also make discoveries of mental and spiritual laws? Indeed, the great discoveries of the future will be in these very realms.

Evolution is an eternal unfoldment. Life reveals itself to whoever is receptive to it. A motion picture would have been a miracle in medieval times, and no doubt the figures on the screen would have been regarded as either gods or devils. The birth of spiritual ideas into the human consciousness meets with three distinct reactions: the orthodox say that God never intended such things to be, else He would have revealed them through His prophets; the materialist laughs at them; the child-like are receptive.

Science, philosophy, intuition and revelation all must unite in an impersonal effort if Truth is to be gained and held. No system of thought can stand which denies human experiences; no religion can be vital which separates humanity from Divinity; nor can any science long maintain its position which denies the spontaneous appearance of volition and will.

A human being is more than matter. There is an inner life higher than the psyche. A human being is mind, soul and body; mental, spiritual and physical; intelligence, volition and will, fused into a coordinated personality, and we each can understand ourselves only from the larger viewpoint. We deal with the real person only when we deal with the whole person. We deal with the whole person only when we deal with the mental, spiritual and physical faculties working in unity.

The Unity of God and the Individual

It is fundamental to the philosophy of Science of Mind and Spirit that there can be no cause without an effect and no effect without a cause, even as there can be no inside without an outside, no outside without an inside, or a stick with only one end.

If we assume the Absolute or First Cause to be pure Intelligence and perfect Consciousness, we must assume that this Consciousness is aware of Itself, since there can be no consciousness unless there is something to be conscious of, to cognize. "The Spirit is the power that knows Itself" is one of the oldest sayings, and since the individual unit, or person, is self-conscious, how much more so must be the Infinite Mind?

We cannot grasp the meaning of Infinite Consciousness nor fathom Its depths, but we argue from the known to the unknown, from our own minds, with their intelligent consciousness, to an Absolute Intelligence, which inter-spheres everything and is manifest through everything—this Absolute Intelligence is the First Cause or that by which everything is made manifest.

All creation, ourselves included, is the result of the contemplation of this First Cause within and upon Itself. In taking form It gives form to the formless, thus expressing the reality of Its own contemplation, which expression of reality through any particular form produces the element of time, which Dean Inge tells us is a sequence of events in a unitary whole.

While neither time nor space are things of themselves, each exists as a necessary complement to the self-knowing mind, which would be unexpressed without time and space.

Could we understand Absolute Causation we should perceive it to be pure Intelligence operating through perfect law and producing perfect effects, which live and have their being not by virtue of an isolated life, but by reason of a universal livingness which permeates all things. We should then see that the world of multiplicity is deeply rooted in a universe of unity; that nothing can happen by chance; that we live under a government of law, from the vast planetary systems to the "garden of roses," from the Archangel, the Christ, to the saint and the sinner, through good and in what we call evil; through cosmic activities and in human destinies we behold the vast objective panorama of invisible but adequate subjective causes.

As we contemplate the mysteries of nature in this panoramic view of objective life, we are amazed at the infinite variations, the complete individualizations and the uniqueness of everything. Here again we are brought to the realization that the Infinite is indeed Infinite, and that within this One there is ample room for individual expressions in the things created.

Each is rooted in the whole, and the Divine Nature manifests through everything. The spontaneity of our inner perceptions which enable us to know truth, either through experiment or by pure intuition, is ample guarantee that humanity is akin to divinity, and that within every person God is concealed, waiting to be revealed through purpose, thought and act.

Within our nature is a reality which knows no difference between itself and the Great Self. It is this indwelling "I" which Jesus referred to as the Father *indwelling him.* Since this real "I" must be perfect and can produce only perfect effects it follows that perfect cause already inheres, not alone in the Divine but also in the human since the human is divine. Somewhere within is the mount from whose lofty peak "the eye beholds the world as one vast plane and one boundless reach of sky." From this inner visioning and our reactions to it flows the power of our lives.

The whole aim of the study of Science of Mind is to realize and consciously penetrate the upper atmosphere of our thought and bring down, as it were, into the lower mind greater visions of reality. Effect follows cause as the night the day, and should we image forth an adequate concept of substance, we would be supplied with all human needs; could we sense perfect being we should experience perfect living; could we reach that serene contemplation of the soul which views all as an undivided part of the Great Self we should no longer be disturbed in our thought.

Health, happiness and success are effects and not causes. Occult and esoteric practices are neither necessary nor beneficial in this work. Any state bordering on trance or hypnotism through self-suggestion is far removed from the field of reality where the consciousness should ever be aware, and still more aware of itself and its unity with the Whole.

Each person is a center of self-conscious life; God is the Life Principle animating us. While this Life Principle is forever hidden from our objective view, we are continuously conscious of Its existence in us and animating all nature. The relationship between the Life Principle and that which It sustains is self-evidently one of unity. The highest perception of humankind has been our sense of this inner oneness with the Spirit. The more completely we become conscious of this Divine union, the more power we have over our own existence, but we should not limit the unity of God and person to the religious field alone, for this has been one of the great mistakes of the ages.

We should not separate life from living, Spirit from matter, nor Divine Principle from a universal creation. God is "all in all"; that is, God *is,* and is in everything. The gardener finds a divine idea concealed in the seed; loosed into action this idea produces a plant. The geologist finds the imprint of invisible forces in the rock. The evolutionist reads the history of cosmic activities on this planet as he or she deciphers the unfolding of an Intelligent Life Force carrying creation forward to its consummating point here, which is the production of self-conscious life. The scientist finds an energy concealed in the atom, and the spiritual genius discloses an intuitive knowledge which can be accounted for only on the theory that we lie in the lap of an Infinite Intelligence.

So close is the union of creation with the Creator that it is impossible to say where one begins and the other leaves off. Emerson tells us that nature is Spirit reduced to Its greatest thinness, and Spinoza says that mind and matter are the same thing, while Jesus boldly proclaimed that the very words which he spoke were Spirit and were life. Brother Lawrence, a Carmelite lay brother of the 1600s noted for his prayerful life, reached a stage of perception where it was impossible for him to pick up a straw without realizing that it was God acting through him. Robert Browning writes of a spark which we may desecrate but never quite lose, and he further proclaims that all are gods, though in the germ. Wordsworth sings that heaven is the native home of all mankind, and Tennyson exclaims that more things are wrought by prayer than this world dreams. Shakespeare perceived sermons in stones and good in everything.

We are on the verge of disclosing a spiritual universe and will ultimately conclude that what we call the material universe is a spontaneous emergence, through evolution, of inner forces which cannot be explained but which must be accepted. How, then, can we doubt that the very mind which we now use is the Intelligent Principle from which all that lives draws its power to be and to express?

In mental treatment this sense of our union with the Divine Mind constitutes the power of the spoken word. Jesus proclaimed, "It is not I but the Father who dwelleth in me, He doeth the works."

The Mystical Marriage is the recognition of this inner

union. "Thy Maker is thy husband" is a proclamation of an Eternal Oneness. "Wilt thou be made whole?" is the question which this inner Principle places before the intellect. Who can answer the riddle of the Universe? The silent sphinx obstructs our pathway until the question is answered.

When the isolated sense of separation melts into one of unity, the riddle is solved and the menacing monster becomes an obedient servant. "Come unto me all ye that are weary and heavy laden and I will give you rest" is an invitation of an Invisible Host, revealing Itself through the mind of one whose eyes were open.

The furtherance of evolution depends upon our ability to sense a unity with nature and her forces. When the knowledge of this unity comes alike to all people, the tread of armies will cease and the bugle call will echo the soft notes of brotherly love. In mental and spiritual healing, the supremely important thing to emphasize is the presence of good and its perfect unity with the individual.

Law, the Servant of the Word

The subjective law of our being is subject to our conscious use of it; of this fact psychology and mental science have ample proof. The subjective reactions to thought are not volitional. Humankind, as we understand ourselves, is the result of our conscious thoughts and acts, plus our subjective reactions to life, plus that indefinable something which is the Spirit in us. This Spirit emerges through us, is aware of Itself and aware of us.

The subjective mind has no self-consciousness, but is intelligently aware of the direction which it receives. It is an effect rather than a cause, a medium or a way rather than a thing or an entity. It apparently becomes an entity but always by proxy. Having no power of initiation, no self-will or conscious choice, it remains plastic, though creative; a thing to be used; a law which must obey.

Insofar as these foregoing statements are understood, they seem provable; how far-reaching the possibilities inherent in these thoughts may be, no one can state. Everything happens as though they were true, hence we have a perfect right to accept them and proceed on this basis.

It is generally accepted that subjective mind is the silent builder of the body, the seat of memory and the repository of thought and emotion. This inner consciousness is the medium between thought and its manifestation.

Unconscious of itself, it is still conscious of what it is doing; unknowing within itself, it yet knows how to do; impersonal by nature, it takes the imprint of personality; neutral, it has no choice; plastic and receptive, it must reflect; acting in accord with natural law as intelligent, creative energy, it brings a creative genius to bear upon the word, far transcending that of the conscious intellect of the entire human race.

It seems a paradox that the conscious mind can direct an intelligence greater than itself, which intelligence neither knows that it is power, nor that it is intelligence;

and yet, are we not constantly using such powers? Who knows how the egg becomes a chicken? Who knows how solid and liquid foods convert themselves into blood, bone and tissue? And yet we know that they do.

When we arrive at the nature of things, there is nothing to do but to press forward with faith in its reliability. The metaphysician will go further than the psychologist and proclaim a universal subjectivity of which our individual subjectivities are but personal uses. This greater subjective mind is the universal principle of all thought and action. It is the silent creator of destiny, having intelligent receptivity and creative ability, yet having no purpose of its own to execute, compelled by its very nature to be a servant of the Spirit.

It is through a use of this greater medium that the Religious Scientist operates. Faith set in motion in this medium produces facts in human experience. Our own individual subjective states of thought constitute the medium through which this law works. If we have a true conviction which is in line with the ultimate harmony, we can create an idea which must clothe itself in a form equal to our mental equivalent of such an idea.

When we wish to demonstrate these principles, we should act as though they were true. We should daily affirm the presence of a Divine Law which obeys our word, insofar as this word is in harmony with the truth. The only limitation set on this word is the limitation of unbelief and the impossibility of using the universal law destructively without ultimately harming the one using it.

When our will and purpose are in line with the Divine will and purpose, we cannot use this law destructively. We have a perfect right to use it for personal advancement and to bring happiness and success into our experience. We should use this law definitely and with full assurance that this seed of conscious thought will be received by a creative intelligence which will produce a harvest that we can reap in due season.

This Universal Subjective Mind exists to us only as a latent possibility until we specialize It. Like other energies of nature, It is something to be used. The declaration that It exists and that we believe in Its possibilities is merely a statement of principles, a proclamation of our faith in the responsiveness of nature to the needs of humankind; but a proclamation of faith never built a house nor drove an automobile—"faith without works is dead." The uncultivated desert remains a wasteland; an image uncaught by the purposive will often degenerates into idle daydreaming and futile fancy.

The laws of nature should be consciously used, definitely specialized. When we have freed ourselves from superstitions regarding mental and spiritual things, we shall be ready to approach them intelligently and incorporate them in our everyday living. This the student of

Science of Mind should daily seek to do. Since we have a creative intelligence, we should use it. As we are surrounded by a mental principle which reacts to our thought, we should consciously set it in motion for definite purposes. Treatment is the act, the art and the science of specializing the universal Law of Mind for specific and individual purposes.

The Law is, but it must be used. Until the time comes when we use it consciously and constructively, we shall be using it unconsciously and perhaps destructively; every time we think, we use this law. We should begin by weeding out all negative states of thought and learn to speak a straight affirmative language. The universe gives *to* us *through* us. All natural laws await the intelligent, guiding hand.

To believe that we are continuously guided in our acts by a Supreme Intelligence is a better state of mind and more productive of good than to believe we are subject to the caprice of fate. Our fate is within our own minds; destiny is but the objective manifestation of subjective mental states. Success and failure are not things of themselves, they are simply modes of expressing the Original Thing. Thought should be daily directed and consciously controlled.

It is written that God's words are "yea and amen," which means that the Infinite does not argue, but meets every person's approach directly, responding to

every person's thought. The material scientist readily
acknowledges a reign of law. The forces of nature are
not coerced, they are directed; so the powers of mind
and spirit are not commanded but commandeered. The
universal flow is forever taking place, the turning of this
flow into the channels of constructive thought is an individual act; thus we specialize a natural energy and utilize a power which otherwise remains chaotic in our
individual lives.

The simplest approach is always the most direct—
"Believe and it shall be done," accept and let it be done;
convince the mind and no longer deny the greater possibility. "Act as though I am and I will be." We must
abandon our ideas to the Supreme Cause and wait for
the harvest time with joyful expectancy.

There should be a definite and conscious expectancy;
we should feel as though the entire power of the universe
were for us and never against us; all conversation to the
contrary must be resolutely set aside. Remember that
mental treatment is neither wishing nor willing; it is an
affirmation of the presence, the power and the willingness
of the Divine Law to specialize Itself for us, to meet every
human need. It is not through human determination, nor
by "power or by might," but by the silent workings of the
Spirit through organized thought that the Divine imparts
Its power to each person. We are chemists in the
laboratory of the Infinite; what shall we produce?

The Energy Back of Thought

Nature lies in the lap of an Intelligence and Life, which, without any apparent effort on Its own part, provides both seedtime and harvest. How can we doubt that the power back of things is adequate and is a Unity?

Originality, spontaneity and volition crop out at every point in nature; we can see but one reasonable conclusion, that back of everything—coordinating everything—is a Unitary Power, all-knowing, all-wise, all-good, all-beautiful, absolute, birthless, deathless and changeless.

Our popular religions, with their half-gods, are but different resting places of the mind—inns where the weary soul rests overnight on its journey from the outer circumference of materialism to an inner consciousness of idealism; at the dawn of a greater vision, with the dew of Eternity on the garden, the soul ventures forth to find a better God.

Our half-concepts come *as* we need them and remain *while* we need them, to be finally lost in a *greater* concept of Reality. Every person's religion is an answer to the cry of the soul for something which is real, something which may be relied upon—a resting place for which everyone instinctively feels a need.

We are created, we are told, in the likeness of the Eternal, after the image of the Infinite. We sense a divinity within, a nature hidden in the cryptic interior of our minds which we have scarcely penetrated—a unity with the Whole. The intuitive faculty which we use to uncover Reality is evidence that this Reality is already latent within us.

It matters not if we reach this place through the inductive process of science or by the deductive process of revelation. It is useless for the materialist to say that revelation is a myth, for it can be shown that science is an inductive process leading to deductions, and that all deductions are revelations. All life is a revelation—from the cradle to the grave; by revelation is meant the uncovering of that which *already is* in essence, law and order.

The most penetrating and far-reaching conclusions ever made by humankind have announced that creation is a result of the contemplation of God. The Law of the Universe propels Mind into action, action into creation—creation being an effect, a result. The creative word of Universal Intelligence projects Itself into form. When we speak of the energy back of thought, or the power of faith and prayer, we are not thinking of will-power, but of Original Power. The thought, or the prayer, merely uses an energy which already is. The electrician does not put energy into electricity, but he takes it out.

If there is a law of thought, if there is evidence that any prayer was ever answered or that any person's faith has consummated in an objective realization of that faith, then there is evidence of an Intelligence in the universe which accepts the word of faith and acts upon it.

Intelligent practitioners know that there is a Universal Law which acts on our word, and we use this Law with the definite knowledge that we are scientifically using a proven principle, a known, definite and provable force; for to us the presence of an Intelligent Power in the universe, which receives the impress of this thought and acts upon it, is an accepted and proven fact.

The practitioner knows, however, that this energy can only respond by correspondence. In other words: the measure of our faith in the Infinite is the measure of our capacity to draw from the Infinite; this is why the Great Teacher said: "It is done unto you as you believe." If we can believe in a great good, then much good can come to us. It is according to our mental acceptance, or mental equivalents—according to our faith—that life manifests through us.

We measure life through our concept; automatically, thought has power. If we wish to prove that there is a spiritual principle which we may definitely use, let us forego any sense of coercion and become as a little child in receptivity; let us definitely and consciously accept our good and continue accepting until we experience it. We must subject ourselves to the Law if we wish the Law to subject Itself to us. A good-natured flexibility with one's self, and a faith, persisting in the face of anything which would contradict it, is the only way to approach the principle of right action.

Deeper than our mind is the Spirit, which we but slightly comprehend. From this Universal Reservoir a power passes through our minds into action. When the mind is peaceful and still, it catches a vision of this greater good; while the mind is in turmoil and combat, it cannot receive an image beyond the limiting circle of the small measure in which it has been treading around. Somewhere, the walls of experience must be broken down; we must learn that we can transcend our previous experiences, that behind the finite is the Infinite.

We shall not arrive at the point of demonstration while we believe it is necessary to put energy into Spirit, thus usurping the throne of the Original Creative Genius. There is an energy in thought, not because we will it to be so, but because it is so. Definite thinking draws this energy to our conscious desires and demonstrates at the level of our faith in the law of God.

There must be a conscious belief on the part of those seeking to demonstrate this Principle that their faith and thought are but the avenues through which the law expresses itself to them. In the technique of mental treatment, thought merely uses the power intelligently. The will decides how the power is to be used. If we have a problem to solve we must know that Intelligence is now solving it; this is to be remembered when giving a mental treatment. The treatment should be concrete, specific, conscious, definite, embodying the general ideas which one wishes to bring into objectification.

While there is a point of decision and choice in treatment, there must be no outline; if the treatment is the cause, the demonstration is the effect and is already in the cause, as the flower is in the seed. It is written: "I am the Alpha and the Omega." Treatment should be given with a complete acceptance that there is a power, an Intelligence and a law which operates upon the word; whatever the mind holds which denies this acceptance should be consciously neutralized, clearing the field of doubt and leaving the mind open to the Cause.

One definite experience which proves the integrity of the soul and its direct relationship to the Universal Mind and spirit will do more good than all the teachings of theology, for thus alone can we arrive at the place where we can say: "This I know, whereas I was blind, now I see."

The Energy back of constructive thought is Spirit; Spirit permeates everything; hence, constructive thought calls the best out of any particular experience. A Religious Scientist is a practical idealist, but not a dreamer. Thought swings from contemplation into action, from prayer into performance, for while there is in the innermost recesses of our soul a place which dwells in eternal stillness and inaction, there is also a place at the circumference of our being which, animated by this inner principle, goes forth to accomplish. Thus alone can contemplation become fruition, and inner recognition outer realization.

It would not be correct practice to spend one's whole time contemplating or meditating. There should be a balance between the inner and the outer states; from an inner communion of the soul with the Spirit there comes inspiration and guidance, but this inner state would remain an idle dream unless heaven were brought to earth, and spiritual perception woven into the fabric of everyday experience.

It has been said that the "kingdom of good" will be realized on earth when the without shall become as the within. "Thy will be done, thy kingdom come on earth as it is in heaven" is a recognition of the unity which takes place when the real is linked to the ideal. It is then that experience becomes a legitimate offspring, in the outer world, of inner states of happiness and well-being.

An unexpressed person is incomplete. The objective universe, through which alone we interpret the Invisible Cause, is evidence enough that the Original Creative Genius forever passes from substance, through Law, into manifestation. We would defeat the very purpose of life should we live in a continuous state of meditation or prayer, oblivious to the objective world. The practical values of spiritual perception remain latent until objectified. Any attempt to isolate one's self from the world of action is contrary to the order of the universe, therefore futile. As practical religionists, we seek to make our dreams come true, and unless our dreams are subjective hallucinations, they will become actual experiences if we demonstrate our principle, which is, that true ideas pass through into accomplishment.

Unless we are engaged in spiritual and mental practice, we need not spend more than thirty minutes or an hour each day in meditation, but this amount of time is of inestimable value in our practical life, for it is here that we join the real to the ideal and receive inspiration for action and guidance toward accomplishment. In actual practice, we try to sense the union of the Spirit with everything we are doing, and as there is "no great and no small to the Soul that maketh all," it follows that our slightest desire is important to the universe, since it is some expression of the Parent Mind through us. This gives a dignity to our slightest undertaking, and places a greater value on human endeavors. The happiness of the individual life is essential to the Universal Wholeness, for thus alone can It find an extension of Itself.

As we seek to demonstrate the power of spiritual realization in our everyday affairs, we should think of ourselves as being Divinely guided, affirming that our mind is continually impressed with the images of right action, and that everything in our life is controlled by love, harmony and peace; that everything we do prospers, and that the eternal energy back of all things animates everything which we undertake. Every objective evidence to the contrary should be resolutely denied, and, in its place, should come a sense of right action. We should feel a unity of the Spirit in us with the Spirit in all people and running through all events. We should definitely declare that the Spirit within us is the Spirit of God, quickening into right action everything which we touch, bringing the best out of all our experiences, forever guiding and sustaining. The greatest good which our mind is able to conceive should be affirmed as a part of our everyday experience. From such daily meditation, we should venture forth into a life of action with the will to do, the determination to be and a joy in becoming.

Spiritual Evolution

The evolution of humankind is definite, unhurried and purposeful. This purposefulness is proven by the fact that something is evolving in a definite manner. There is intent behind the life of the individual. It makes no difference what the process is through which this intent is working. It matters not whether we intuitively conclude ourselves to be the offspring of a Divine Consciousness, or whether we take the more painstaking process and trace our pedigree back to its first movement, we shall arrive at the same conclusion: that something definite is taking place.

"Beloved, now are we the sons of God, and it doth

not yet appear what we shall be, but we know that when He shall appear we shall be like Him, for we shall see Him as He is." The writer was referring to the Christ idea, the universal sonship, the God-intended person, set before us in the Christian Scriptures as the Christ, the ideal person. We are told that all are members of one body which is the Christ, the Son begotten of the only Father, "and it doth not yet appear what we shall be, but we know that when He shall appear we shall be like Him, for we shall see Him as He is." And yet it says, "Beloved, *now* are we the sons of God"—even though the process of evolution is still taking place and has not stopped, and perhaps never will stop, because we shall always unfold. We are now, though, in a state of incompletion—the children of God, and as we more completely evolve we shall see the Christ appear, and "when He shall appear we shall be like Him; for we shall see Him as He is," being transformed from glory unto glory by reason of that divine urge hidden within each of us.

The writer was talking to his associates and saying: Do not fear, you are now the sons of God; do not worry, it is necessarily so; as your consciousness expands you will understand what true sonship means, what God is, what divine sonship means; as you awaken you will realize that you are awakening to yourself. When He shall appear we shall know Him because we shall be like Him. This is the message he was trying to convey, that even now the divine reality is accomplished in the Infinite Mind. "Beloved, now are we the children of God." In other words, within each one of us is an indestructible, an eternal person, a spiritual person, a God-intended person. So we are told to be transformed by the renewing of our minds, by the putting off of the old person and the putting on of the new, which is Christ–the God-intended person.

As we trace the unfoldment of human personality, we find a calm, unhurried, definite and irresistible impulse, building finer forms and more intelligent avenues of self-expression, coming up through all the stages of unconscious and simple conscious organisms until at last it reaches a cycle which ushers in self-conscious humankind. A very definite step takes place when we come to self-conscious humanity. The Divine Spirit has evolved a living soul, an emanation of Itself, that this soul may become immortal but individualized.

Why is it necessary that the soul shall undergo the experiences of evolution? Individuality means spontaneity, self-choice, volition, reality, creative ability. If we were to assume individuality, and volition, without law to bring its choice into fruition, we would have a dream, a hallucination, a fantasy. Individuality presupposes choice, which presupposes the possibility of bringing choice into actual experience. Only through experience can it come full-orbed into conscious unity with the

Divine Mind. When the working idea emerges from an unconscious to a self-conscious state, it becomes individualized. At the doorway of self-choice, arbitrary methods of evolution cease. As we come to the point where we know ourselves, we are individualized; the Cosmic Mind must now wait for us to recognize our relationship to It.

When we reach self-consciousness, the Spirit can do nothing more for us until we consciously cooperate with It. Since human beings first said, "I am," nothing has been forced upon us. We have lived, learned, experienced and discovered.

Nature has awaited our discovery of its laws; as we discover new ones we use them. This is the meaning of an ancient saying, "nature obeys us as we first obey it." We must come to understand her laws, then she will obey us. Moses knew nothing about electricity; Solomon, with all his wisdom, had no automobile to ride in, yet all these possibilities existed—waiting— "Behold I stand at the door and knock." Just as soon as the Divine Mind has brought the evolution of personality to a point of self-recognition, it must wait on our conscious cooperation for further evolution.

But from the beginning, the idea of humankind perfected must have been in the Divine Mind; involved within the cause is always the effect. And in the mind of the Eternal, *humankind* must be perfect. God is perfect

Mind and cannot conceive imperfect ideas, hence the idea of humankind as held in the mind of God must be a perfect idea. The perfect human is the only human God knows.

Humankind may do as it wills with itself, but it will always have itself left. We may desecrate, but we can never lose our lives. The Spirit ever has a witness within us, and the God-intended person already knows that he or she is one with the whole; that nature is comprised of one ultimate power, using many instruments and having many avenues of expression. The time has come in our evolution when we should awaken to a recognition that behind each one stands the eternal Mind, that each has complete access to It; that each may come to It for inspiration and revelation; that surrounding all is a Divine Law obeying the dictates of this eternal Mind.

The unfoldment of consciousness has arrived at the place where individuality can realize its own divinity. We are waking to the recognition of this. The God-intended person is a divine center of God-consciousness on the pathway of experience for the purpose of evolving a definite individuality. But it is only as we work in conscious cooperation with the Universal that we awaken to Reality. It is only as we understand nature and comply with her laws that we can ever hope to use them. The law is one of freedom and not of bondage. Behind all, there is a great urge trying to express through every medium; why not allow it to express through us?

Evolution is a principle, which, though invisible, finds manifestation in every form of life. It is the logical and necessary outcome of Universal Intelligence or Spirit. But evolution is an effect of intelligence and not its cause; it follows involution. Involution is the idea while evolution is the unfoldment of the idea. Involution pre-cedes evolution with mechanical precision propelled by an immutable law—the Law of Cause and Effect.

God is Universal Intelligence or Spirit. The only way that Universal Intelligence can move is by an interior movement. God must move within God if God is all; He moves *within* and *upon* Himself. The movement back of the objective world must be a subjective movement, a movement of consciousness. It is necessary, then, that whatever movement takes place *must* take place within and upon the One. And it follows that whatever is cre-ated is created out of this One.

God moves upon God. This is the starting point of creation. Every time one conceives an idea, that is God expressing Itself. It is eternally knowing and eternally known through everyone. God's nature is to know. There is an emotional craving or desire for expression inherent in the universe.

There is a universal law obeying the will of Spirit. This is the law through which that which is involved, evolves. We, as conscious spirit, set a universal law in motion which makes things from ideas. The spirit *involves,* the law *evolves;* the law does not know that it is evolving, it is its nature to evolve.

Evolution, then, is not a thing of itself. It is an effect. Behind all objective form there is a subjective likeness which exactly balances, and is the prototype of, the form. The thing involved perfectly balances the thing evolving from it. Evolution is the time and the process through which the Spirit unfolds. Insofar as any individual understands this mental law, he or she is able to use it. We must learn *how* it works and comply with the *way* it works; always it is an obedient servant. As we sow, so shall we also reap. Involution and evolution, the thought and the thing, the word and the law, the purpose and the execution—this is the sequence of the way the law works.

While there is liberty in the evolving principle, it is always in accord with certain fundamental laws of necessity. It seems as though behind evolution there is an irresistible pressure, compelling more, better, higher and greater things.

If we study the evolution of locomotion from the rising of humankind from the clod, we see people riding upon a horse, in a cart, then in a wagon, and so on to the automobile and the airplane. What is this but the evolution of locomotion, the unfolding through the human mind of the possibility of travel? If we watch the evolution of travel by water, we find the same thing from the raft to the ship.

What is the inevitable end of locomotion? We shall ultimately do away with every visible means of transportation. That which is the principle back of evolution will not be satisfied with the process through which we now go. When we shall have unified with Omnipresence, we shall be omnipresent.

When you and I know enough and are in Los Angeles and wish to be in San Francisco, we shall be there. When we know enough to want to pass on to another plane of existence and come back again, we shall be able to do so. When we know enough to multiply the loaves and fishes, we shall do so. When we know enough to walk on the water, we shall be able to do that, and it will all be in accord with natural law in a spiritual world.

READER/CUSTOMER CARE SURVEY

We care about your opinions. Please take a moment to fill out this Reader Survey card and mail it back to us.
As a special **"thank you"** we'll send you exciting news about interesting books and a valuable **Gift Certificate.**

Please PRINT using ALL CAPS

Name	First	MI.	Last Name
Address			
City		ST	Zip
Phone # ( ) —		Fax # ( ) —	
Email			

(1) Gender:
____ Female ____ Male

(2) Age:
____ 12 or under ____ 40-59
____ 13-19 ____ 60+
____ 20-39

(3) Marital Status
____ Married
____ Single
____ Divorced/Widowed

(4) Did you receive this book as a gift?
____ Yes ____ No

(5) How many Health Communications books have you bought or read?
____ 1 ____ 2-4 ____ 5+

(6) How did you find out about this book?
Please fill in ONE.
1) ____ Recommendation
2) ____ Store Display
3) ____ Bestseller List
4) ____ Online
5) ____ Advertisement
6) ____ Catalog/Mailing
7) ____ Interview/Review (TV, Radio, Print)

(7) Where do you usually buy books?
Please fill in your top TWO choices.
1) ____ Bookstore
2) ____ Religious Bookstore
3) ____ Online
4) ____ Book Club/Mail Order
5) ____ Price Club (Costco, Sam's Club, etc.)
6) ____ Retail Store (Target, Wal-Mart, etc.)

(9) What subjects do you enjoy reading about most? Rank only **FIVE**. Use 1 for your favorite, 2 for second favorite, etc.

	1	2	3	4	5
1) Parenting/Family	○	○	○	○	○
2) Relationships	○	○	○	○	○
3) Recovery/Addictions	○	○	○	○	○
4) Health/Nutrition	○	○	○	○	○
5) Christianity	○	○	○	○	○
6) Spirituality/Inspiration	○	○	○	○	○
7) Business Self-Help	○	○	○	○	○
8) Teen Issues	○	○	○	○	○
9) Sports	○	○	○	○	○

(14) What attracts you most to a book?
(Please rank 1-4 in order of preference.)

	1	2	3	4
1) Title	○	○	○	○
2) Cover Design	○	○	○	○
3) Author	○	○	○	○

TAPE IN MIDDLE; DO NOT STAPLE

BUSINESS REPLY MAIL
FIRST-CLASS MAIL PERMIT NO 45 DEERFIELD BEACH, FL

POSTAGE WILL BE PAID BY ADDRESSEE

HEALTH COMMUNICATIONS, INC.
3201 SW 15TH STREET
DEERFIELD BEACH FL 33442-9875

FOLD HERE

Comments:

The Secret of Spiritual Power

7

By Spiritual Power I mean a dynamic something which is intelligent, conscious of what it is doing and able to do it without any external aid. We think of physical energy in terms of horsepower or the ability to lift a weight a certain number of feet from the earth. Let us think of Spiritual Power not as contradicting physical power, but as being more subtle. There must be spiritual power which does not contradict the physical, but is the parent of it—being the greater, it must include the lesser.

Through the ages there are authentic records of persons who have exercised spiritual power, no matter what their religion or theology may have been. No one can be a student of history, or a keen observer of life, without coming to realize that there is such a thing as spiritual power. Therefore, without argument, we may accept its reality.

All the world is in search of Reality. Intuitively we feel the necessity of Something greater than we are, Something upon which we may rely with certainty. We need spiritual power even more than we need physical power. We need both and we have both. But having great physical energy at our command has not satisfied us. Consequently, we see an interesting thing going on in the world today—many of our scientists are becoming philosophers endeavoring to determine the relationship of their own science to the larger meaning of life. One of the world's greatest psychologists says that after thirty years spent in analyzing the subjective thought of educated people from every part of the world he has found, in the case of people over thirty-five years of age, that almost without exception the neurosis is caused by the lack of a true religious perception. He is not speaking as the theologian, but as a scientist and a physician, when he states that in no case has there been a permanent healing without the restoration of some type of religious faith.

His conclusions have nothing to do with any particular creed, doctrine or dogma. He is speaking of the

essence of a true religious conviction which relates neither to Catholic nor Protestant, Jew nor Gentile. It
means an inner conviction which is truly spiritual, no
matter what outward form of worship it takes. Religion
is a reaction to humanity's spiritual inquiry, the outward
form of an inner conviction. But all through the ages
those who have been truly spiritual, no matter what outward form their conviction took, have had this in common; they have believed in something greater than they
were, and a something which responded to them. This
belief is the very basis of spiritual power; it is the fundamental principle of every religion. We do not need
to discuss the merits or demerits of other people's
religions.

Every person's religion is good and necessary to him
or her, or he or she would not have it. We like ours, that
is why we espouse its cause. The power of all religions
is in the spiritual principles involved and in our conscious unity with these principles. There is such a thing
as spiritual power.

But what shall we do with the people who are so full
of common sense that it fairly oozes out of them? They
are, perhaps, in many ways very scientific people, probably marvelous mathematicians, who may know all
about the physiological structure of the anatomy, but
with it all they are so full of common sense that it has
become a disease with them. They are so sane that they

are almost insane. "Show me the Soul," they exclaim, yet they have not the slightest idea what the energy is that enables them to ask this question. All the physicists on earth do not know what the power is that enables us to wiggle our finger. If we should wait for that which is objectively tangible before we deduce a principle, we would never get anywhere. There is no law in the Universe which has this kind of tangibility. There is some intangible reality which constitutes the dynamics of spiritual power. It is always the invisible that gives rise to the visible.

Let us never fall into the grave error of thinking it is a mark of intelligence to say, "I am so sensible that I must have everything made tangible." There is nothing more tangible in the universe than thought, and who has ever seen thought? Love cannot be seen: We see what people do who are in love—we see that it changes their whole psychology, and generally for the better, but it is an intangible thing. We do not see life; we experience it. Therefore, we need not be confused if someone asks, "What does Spiritual Power look like? Have you weighed and measured it?" Of course not!

We have heard a great deal about the psyche and repressions, complexes and inhibitions and the libido. Yet there is nothing about them that we can get a picture of; they are invisible and intangible. Who has ever seen the power or the intelligence that converts bread, potatoes and meat into fingernails—and yet here they are.

So let us feel that when we are discussing spiritual power we are talking about something that is real. We have more evidence of the Soul than we have of the atom. Much was known about the soul before we ever heard of the atom. Actually, matter disappears into an entirely theoretical and hypothetical field and no one knows what it is.

Through the ages there have been people like Jesus, Buddha, Emerson—like many saints of the Catholic and Protestant churches (and many saints who had no church)—who have had, and used, a subtle spiritual power. So far, psychology has not accounted for this Power; the pursuit of philosophy is a search for it. Most scientific research has overlooked it, but it is the very essence of religion and its highest goal, a union with some invisible but intelligent reality to which we have given the name of God or Spirit. The approach of innumerable people to Reality has produced a corresponding response and reaction from whatever it is they have contacted, which is just as tangible as a cornfield at harvest time or as a sunset.

We are just emerging from an age of such extreme scientificism that it almost produced a spiritual stagnation of the soul. People thought that because everything could be resolved into Law, nothing spiritual was left. That age is passing. It was perhaps necessary in order to usher in the remarkable things science has done for us. But we need scientists who are able to ponder deeply on the meaning of their own discoveries. Why is it that all scientific research leads back into that invisible Source of Nature from which all things spring? It seems as though the end of all the sciences converge in the beginning of an infinite unity from which each one must emerge. This is a belief of many scientific people of our day.

Should it seem strange, then, that we who are engaged in the search of self-discovery should say that the spirit of humanity is rooted in a common unity, one universal Presence? Surely we have an adequate foundation upon which to build not the hope, but the assurance that "each one of us is a God-thought in the germ."

The secret of spiritual power is a consciousness of one's union with the whole and the availability of good. We are one with a universal creativeness which is the God of theology, the Spirit of mysticism, the Reality of philosophy and the Principle of science. God is accessible to all people.

Let us approach this Reality in a childlike manner. We shall then wave aside all differences and realize that Jew or Gentile, Protestant or Catholic, Buddhist or Confucianist, idealist or agnostic, all have a spiritual power in such degree as they are unified with Reality. The history of spiritual endeavor has proved that when one believes in spiritual reality it descends into his or her thought and flows out into expression. This is why people like Jesus have said, "Believe!"

I have often felt that the Spirit must be pure belief, pure imagination, pure feeling, perfect volition and complete knowingness, fused into a unity. An infinite personalness, as personal to you and to me as we are to each other. God must be more than a mathematical principle. Spirit is the Cause, the essence of that Being from which we are personified. In that place where the Spirit personifies, it must be personal to us, not separate from us, but personal and present *in us*. Perhaps this is the meaning of these sayings—"It is not I but the Father who dwelleth in me" or "The Father is greater than I."

Spiritual power arises from a consciousness of our unity with the whole and an awareness of the direct responsiveness of the Spirit to us. Its creativeness being with and in us, it is ever available, not as "some far-off Divine event toward which the whole Creation moves," but as that thing Whitman meant when he said that within each of us nestles the seed of perfection. And what Emerson meant when he said that Jove nods to Jove behind each one of us. It is the thing all spiritual enlightenment has recognized—God incarnated in the individual. As Emerson said, "Let us not say God was, but is: not God spake, but speaks."

The immediate availability of the presence of Spirit is

"neither in the mountain nor at the temple: neither lo here nor lo there—for behold the Kingdom of God is within you." This is a perception of spiritual power. Therefore, when we speak the truth, it is no longer I, but "the Father who dwelleth in me."

Could we thus conceive of the Divine Spirit as being incarnate in us, while at the same time ever being more than that which is incarnated, would we not expand spiritually and intellectually? Life is creative, it is intelligent, it responds to us intelligently. To know *this* is one of the secrets of spiritual power. It is direct. We should believe in eternal goodness, eternal love and eternal responsiveness.

Since our ability to know is God in us, it must follow that thought is creative. "The words I speak unto you, they are spirit and they are life." The teacher did not say these words are going to stir up the pity of God; he said, "*These words,*" and then he sent out his word which healed. When thought knows, understands and embodies Reality, it becomes and is Reality, and Reality is power. This is the secret of spiritual treatment. Spiritual healing is not willing, wishing, beseeching, nor repeating a lot of formulas. It is the result of a dawning perception of Spirit, incarnated in the one needing help. When the illusion of opposites disappears from our mental perception and we come to realize that we are whole, we shall be made whole.

I was reading an article a few days ago written by one of the foremost psychologists of our day, in which he said that analytical psychology is effective in such degree as physicians analyze out of themselves the complexes which are in their patients. For about twenty years, I have been teaching that, in spiritual practice, the practitioners must heal themselves of their patients' troubles. Jesus said that we must first cast the beam out of our own eyes. It is necessary for those practicing spiritual healing to heal themselves of the beliefs, the inhibitions or the psychic knots that are conscious and subjective in the thoughts of their patients.

Spiritual practitioners heal themselves of the beliefs which are affecting their patients, and if they are successful, and if the patients accept such healing, the patients will be healed.

I have known analytical psychologists who work for their patients when the patient is absent. This is what we mean by absent treatment. There is no absence in the One Presence, and psychoanalysts analyzing their patients and treating at a distance will get results. In the spiritual world there is no here or there. There is just everywhere. It is at the point of immediacy.

Spiritual power is an interior awareness. Practitioners think or feel their way to a place in their own minds where they perceive that good is immediately available. There is such a thing as spiritual power. It is a happy, wholesome, healthful-minded thing. A person without religious conviction is not normal. The world needs a spiritual revival more than anything else; it does not need that we should all become Methodists or Catholics or Religious Scientists—it needs *spiritual conviction.*

We should spontaneously look to that which is greater than we are and yet of which we are a part: that which is greater than the personal I, but which is forever flowing *through* the personal I. The personal word has power because spirit is power.

How simple! How direct! Should we not consciously practice this, the greatest of all sciences, the purest of all religions, the most intelligent of all philosophies?

On Becoming Receptive to the Divine

8

I was stimulated to discuss this topic through reading an article by a great industrialist in which he states that in his belief we are surrounded by ideas—that we have always been surrounded by ideas, and that if we were receptive to them we should be able to find out anything that we wish to know. But, he says, thinking is the hardest thing in the world. If you can develop thinkers, you can develop people who can do what they wish to do, have what they wish to have and be what they wish to be.

We are surrounded by an Infinite Mind which, should we become receptive to It, could acquaint us with anything and everything. I would like, however, to differentiate between the thought of being surrounded by ideas and the thought of being surrounded by an Infinite Mind. Ideas are the product of mind; hence mind is the father of ideas; there could be no thought without a thinker. I believe that we are surrounded by both ideas and the mind that conceives them, surrounded by an Infinite Intelligence, which is the Mind of God and the potential storehouse of all possible knowledge. This must be true if we are dealing with the Mind of God. This Infinite Mind is the cause of all that is, and the ultimate of all; it is open to us as our thought is receptive to It. So an inventor draws inventive genius from It, a painter, the inspiration to paint. What we draw from this Mind is, of course, poured through the avenues of our own consciousness and interpreted in our act. In this way each is an individualization of the Universal Spirit.

We are striking at the very root of philosophic thought. How is it that the eternal Mind, the One back of everything, can differentiate and personify Itself in numberless ways without changing Its nature? Let us go into the garden where there are a dozen varieties of plants. All come from one creative soil through one law in that soil, all rooted in the same medium, each bringing forth according to the nature of the seed involved. In the same way, Spirit manifests itself through many individuals. No two are alike, each has a unique place in the universe of Mind, each lives in It; without It no one could live, for each individual life is rooted in the well-spring of Eternal Existence. We each contact It through our own mentality in an individual way, drawing from It an expression which satisfies us. For instance, we are surrounded by the idea of beauty; whoever dwells upon beauty tends to become beautiful, there will be a grace and charm expressing itself through that person which no one can fail to recognize and appreciate.

If we make ourselves receptive to the idea of love, we become lovable; to the degree that we embody love, we are love. This is why people who love are loved; it does not pay to hate, hate is a human idea; love is a divine verity. If we make ourselves receptive to the ideas of peace, poise and calm, calling upon these divine reali-ties, we find them flowing through us and we become peaceful, poised and calm. We have mental equilibrium and balance. Try this some day when you feel dis-traught, discouraged, agitated and irritated. Sit down with yourself—for there is a self within you that is real; no one can ever enter here but yourself, for it is you. Therefore, sit with yourself, that you may meet your-self, that the inner self may talk to the outer self; speak to it, calling it peace, if it is peace you need. Say, "Perfect me within me"—just as though you were talking to a per-son—or "My peace within me, which is perfect, come forth and express through me," and musing on this, meditating upon it, being receptive to it—not forcing, not coercing but *allowing*—you will find that the physical body will relax. Your agitation will disappear, confidence and peace will follow, and balance will be gained.

So we might say of other ideas such as life, joy, love, harmony, of any idea we desire to embody. We are dealing with the creative intelligence of the universe. It is the Mind and the Intelligence back of all, through all and in all. It is that without which there could be no *human thinking*. If you are an inventor and do not quite grasp the idea you need, what do you do? Look within yourself for the answer. Say, "Creative, inventive genius within me, the knower, that which I wish to know about this particular thing is now known to me." Make your words specific and direct.

When the Universal Mind flows through the individual, It comes to the surface of the conscious mind as an actual experience. Truth comes from the inner to the outer self, *from* God, the Universal Spirit, *to* God the manifest person; for every person is a direct manifestation of God.

There is a greater mind within each one which may be called upon. There is nothing too small or too great for this Mind. Listen! Be receptive! Believe absolutely! Be convinced! The one with a great purpose in life is always consciously or unconsciously holding this purpose up to the universal influx, thus causing an outpouring of divine wisdom through his or her own individual mind. I believe that all great people have done this. They may not have known or believed that they were doing it, but I think that all who have achieved success in any branch of life have used this power consciously or unconsciously. It makes no difference whether we say ideas come from God or from humanity, for when we get back to the real person we cannot separate that person from God. God, the Universal, individualizes in each person; all are personifications of the same Spirit.

The Spirit is One and not two! It is a perfect Whole. Feel that It expresses Itself directly through you, is your guiding star in every enterprise. "Go not thou in search of him but to thyself repair, wait thou within the silence dim and thou shalt find him there." There is a side to us which lies open to the Infinite. The infinite wisdom becomes human knowledge in such degree as the human furnishes a channel through which it may flow. The greatest people who have ever lived have recognized this fact. They have consciously expected it, consciously accepted it, consciously received it, and there came a time when they consciously felt it flowing through them.

If we need divine guidance we should consciously call for it, saying: "Perfect Spirit within, which cannot be mistaken, acquaint my mind," or, "Let the Infinite

Intelligence within me acquaint my mind, tell me what to do, that it may come forth into personal expression." But bring it through. Do not leave it up in the air; here is the difference between a dreamer and the practical person: the dreamer is always floating around in the clouds; the practical people keep their thought in the clouds and their feet on earth. In this way they bring heaven to earth through themselves; this is necessary. Let us keep the dream side open as it is the beautiful side of our natures; it is the meditative, contemplative side, the subtle side forever merged with the universe and at one with good. Since this inner self is in continuous connection with the outer self, it can cause a flow of intelligence, stimulating the mind and brain to purposefulness, to creative genius, to executive ability. There is something in the most practical which longs for this still, silent presence. When we spend our entire time in objective things, never getting back to the higher self, we are piling brick upon brick, sooner or later to see them fall about us in ruin. The toiler dies in a day unless the dreamer refreshes and invigorates him with that divine influx which comes from the "Inner self which never tires, fed by the deep, eternal fires."

There is a place in us open to the Infinite. But when the Spirit brings Its gift, by pouring Itself through us, It can only give to us what we take; the taking is mental. If we persist in saying, "Life will not give us that which is good," It cannot, for Life must interpret Itself to us through our intelligence.

Let the unhappy call upon joy; it is indwelling. That joy which sings in the dark and dances in the sunlight; the joy of an eternal sense of completion which must be inherent in the Divine Mind. Let us open our consciousness to its influx, that it may enrapture the soul. That joy which Lowell tells us climbs to a soul in the grass and flowers. This joy already is within.

Let the sad and depressed call upon this wellspring of joy within that it may overflow; we cannot be depressed when we contact its surge. Mind rests in action. The Spirit is never weary. God does not have to sleep. Let the one who is depleted in vitality call upon the vital force within; it is life energy. "Perfect life, complete life within me" (not somewhere else), "let that within me which is life, force, power, vitality, come forth." Sense it; listen to it. Receive it. Expect it. Take it.

As this individualization of Spirit takes piece, it penetrates the finite consciousness; it saturates the human personality with the essence of Its own being and radiates a power and reality that is sublime. "Call upon me and I will answer." "Onlook the Deity and the Deity will onlook thee." "Act as though I am and I will be." God—in us, as us—is us. Let us be receptive to the Divine Nature that It may flow into our everyday living. New arts, new sciences, new religions, better government and a higher civilization wait on our thought. The pent-up energy of life and the possibility of human evolution work through our imagination and will. The time is ready; the place is where we are now, and it is done unto all as they really believe and act.

Principle and
Practice

The first principle fundamental to an understanding of mental and spiritual science is that we are surrounded by an Infinite Intelligence. We do not comprehend the meaning of such an Intelligence, except in a very small degree, but because we are intelligent beings we can sense the presence of an Intelligence which is beyond our human comprehension, an Intelligence which is great enough in Its own nature to encompass the past, to understand perfectly the present and to be the creator of the future. It is the cause of everything that has been and is that out of which will unfold everything that is to be. Our own intelligence is one of Its activities and is of like nature to It, the same in essence but not the same in degree.

At the level of our comprehension of ourselves we know God. This self-knowingness, which is also God-knowing, has the possibilities of eternal expansion. As individual intelligences, you and I communicate with each other, can respond to each other; and in so doing we establish the fact that intelligence responds to intelligence. This same law must hold good whether we think of finite intelligence responding to finite intelligence or whether we think of Infinite Intelligence responding to finite intelligence, for intelligence is the same in essence wherever we find it. We may rest assured that Infinite Intelligence responds to us by the very necessity of being true to Its own nature.

But how does It respond? It can respond only by corresponding, which is but another way of saying that the Infinite Intelligence responds to us by the direct impartation of Itself through us. This is the meaning of that mystical saying, "The Highest God and the Innermost God is One God," and the saying of Jesus, "I and the Father are One." Whatever intelligence we possess is some degree, some measure of that Infinite Intelligence which we call God.

The Infinite Mind imparts of Itself to the finite through the act of incarnation. The evolution of the human race is a process whereby Intelligence passes by successive degrees of incarnation, through evolution, into the human mind. While there are different knowledges, each specific knowledge is but a certain way through which we penetrate that Wisdom which comprehends and includes all knowledges and all systems.

The Spirit responds to us by corresponding to our states of thought. We enter into It in such degree as we comprehend It. It enters into us through correspondence in such degree as we comprehend It. Prayer—communion with the Spirit, meditation or contemplation—is for the purpose of unifying our minds with the Universal Mind, opening up the avenues of our thought to a greater influx.

The Spirit is ever ready, ever waiting because it is Its nature to incarnate. The greater our receptivity and comprehension, the more complete Its flow. The Universe is not only a spiritual system, it is an orderly system. We are living under a government of law, always, whether we deal with the soul, the body or the Spirit, whether we are dealing with physics or with metaphysics. The law is subject to the Spirit, which does not mean that the Spirit is capricious and may create a law only to break it, but does mean that law is subject to the Spirit, in that it is Its Servant—just as all the laws of nature are our servants and obey us insofar as we understand them and properly use them. The spirit, being Omniscient, understands and properly uses all law. Hence, the Spirit never contradicts Its own nature, is always harmonious, is complete within Itself; It exists in a state of perpetual bliss and always acts in accord with the law of Its own being.

We are of like nature to this supreme Spirit. Everything exists within It. We exist within It, having arrived at a state of consciousness whereby we can consciously approach It, believe in It, receive It; and in receiving the Spirit, we receive the law which is Its servant, and that law becomes our servant.

We are intelligent beings living in an intelligent universe which responds to our mental states, and, insofar as we learn to control those mental states, we shall automatically control our environment. This is what is meant by the practical application of the principles of Science of Mind to the problems of everyday living. This is what is meant by demonstration.

Naturally our first thought is that we would like to demonstrate health of body, peace of mind, prosperity in our affairs; to neutralize a circumstance which is unhappy or to attract to ourselves some good which we have not been enjoying. Such a desire is natural and in every way normal, and the possibility of such demonstration already exists within the mind of every living soul. Every one of us has within himself or herself the power to consciously cooperate with the spiritual side of our existence in such a way that it will create for us a new body and a new environment and a greater happiness. But the greatest good which this philosophy of life brings to us is a sense of certainty, a sense of the reality of our own soul, of the continuity of our own individualized being and the relationship of this self to the great Whole.

The greatest good that can come to us is the forming of an absolute certainty of ourselves and of our relationship to the Universe, forever removing the sense of heaven as being outside ourselves, the fear of hell or any future state of uncertainty. We are each a part of the life that is, some part of the Eternal God. We are forever reaching out, forever gaining, growing, expanding; Spirit is forever incarnating Itself in us.

Such an understanding teaches us that there can never come a time when we shall stop progressing, that age is an illusion, that limitation is a mistake, that unhappiness is ignorance. We cannot be afraid when we know the truth. The greatest good accompanying such an understanding of truth will be the elimination of fear. This understanding will rob us of our loneliness and give us a sense of security which knows no fear, a peace without which no life can be happy, a poise which is founded on this peace and a power which is the result of the union of peace with poise.

We can be certain that there is an Intelligence in the Universe to which we may come, which will inspire and guide us, a love which overshadows. God is real to the one who believes in the supreme Spirit, real to the soul which senses its unity with the Whole. Every day and every hour we are meeting the eternal realities of life, and in such degree as we cooperate with these eternal realities in love, in peace, in wisdom and in joy, believing and receiving, we are automatically blessed.

It is not by a terrific mental struggle or soul-strain that we arrive at this goal but through a quiet expectation, a joyful anticipation, the calm recognition that all the peace there is and all the power there is and all the good there is is Love, the Living Spirit Almighty.

A mental treatment is a definite act of the conscious mind, setting the law in motion for the one specified in the treatment. A treatment is a spiritual entity in the mental world, fully equipped with the intelligence and the power to demonstrate itself.

When we are giving a treatment, we believe that our word is operated upon by an intelligent, creative agency which has at its disposal the ways, the methods, the means and the inclination to receive our treatment, and to create those circumstances which would be the logical outcome of this treatment.

If we wish to demonstrate supply we would not say, "I am a multimillionaire," but we would seek to realize that Infinite Substance is irresistible supply. We would say to ourself, "I am surrounded by Pure Spirit, perfect

Law, Divine Order, limitless substance which intelligently responds to me. It is not only around me, but it is also in me; it is around and in everything. It is the essence of perfect action. It is perfect action in my affairs. Daily I am guided by this Divine Intelligence, I am not allowed to make mistakes, I am compelled to make the right choice at the right time; there is no confusion in my mind, no doubt whatsoever. I am certain, expectant and receptive."

As the result of statements such as these, we reeducate our mind, re-creating and redirecting the subjective state of our thought. It is the subjective state of our thought which decides what is going to happen to us, and because the subjective state of our thought often contradicts our conscious desires, a sense of doubt arises.

When we affirm the presence of good, this sense of doubt is an echo of previous experiences; it is the judgment according to appearances which we must be careful to avoid. Unless we are conscious that we are dealing with a transcendent and Creative Power, how can we expect to demonstrate at all?

We must never lose sight of this Power. The demonstrations, produced through the scientific use of the power of spiritual thought-force, are a result of the operation of a law which in no way is limited to any present condition. Evolution itself proves this to be self-evident. The one seeking to use this power must have some sense, some inward conviction that he or she is dealing with an originative, creative law.

Why these things are so no one knows, but experience has so repeatedly proven that we can deal with a law which is unconditioned by anything except our unbelief that there need be no question in anyone's mind. It is never a question as to whether the law is able or willing.

The law is both able and willing, and we might say that the only limitations it imposes upon us are these: The law cannot do anything which contradicts the Divine nature or the orderly system through which this Divine nature functions. It must always be true to itself. The law cannot give us anything we cannot mentally and spiritually digest. In these two propositions we find the only limitations imposed upon us by the creative law.

But these are not limitations at all, for we do not wish anything contrary to the Divine nature, nor can we expect either the Spirit or the law to make us a gift we do not accept. We are certain that the Divine Nature is one of goodness, of truth and of beauty, of reason, of love and of kindliness, of sympathy, of understanding and of responsiveness. We feel our own natures to be like unto It, the same in essence, though, of course, not the same in degree.

There is really, then, no limitation outside our own ignorance, and since we all can conceive a greater good than we have so far experienced, we all have within our own minds the ability to transcend previous experiences and rise triumphant over them, but we shall never triumph over them while we persist in going through the same old mental reactions. There is something positive about a good mental treatment, something almost arbitrary, something relentless, unquestioning.

How can there be an acceptance of a greater good unless its spiritual significance rises through our mental equivalents to reach the level of that good? If we are still submerged in doubt and fear, in uncertainty and dread, shall not these monsters need first to be slain before peace and confidence can be gained?

Prayer and Treatment

Faith has been recognized as a power throughout the ages, whether it be faith in God, in one's fellows, in one's self, or in what one is doing. Those who have great faith have great power.

Why is it that one person's prayers are answered while another's remain unanswered? It cannot be because God is a respecter of persons or has greater consideration for one than for another. It must be that all persons, in their approach to Reality, receive results not because of what they believe but in spite of the peculiarities of their belief. It must be the *way* of their belief that makes the difference.

Faith is not a dogma, a creed, or a statement of being. It is a certain mental approach to Reality. It is an affirmative approach as opposed to a negative one. It is agreement as opposed to denial.

The mind can accept or it can reject, but it cannot do both with the same proposition. The mind cannot accept what it rejects, it cannot embody what it denies, it will not accept what it refuses to believe. Prayer, faith and belief are mental attitudes. It is written that "faith shall heal the sick and God shall raise him up." This implies a human act followed by an act of God. It also implies that without such a human act the act of God will not follow. The act of God follows our *faith in God*.

Prayer leads one to a place of mental acceptance, but prayer without faith is ineffectual. Faith elevates the prayer to conviction and acceptance. Where does God come in? God already is in and does not have to come *from* anywhere *to* anywhere. God is the entire process, both in our thought as individuals and in the universal as answering our individual thought. The prayer of faith makes it possible for the law to respond and do the thing desired. This is a natural law in the spiritual world. We need not be afraid of leaving the Spirit out of the process, for It is Cause, Medium and Effect. The All in All.

The universe is a Spiritual System. Its laws are those of intelligence. We approach it through the mind, which is that part of us that enables us to know, will and act. Prayer is a mental approach to a Reality which is a thing of intelligence. This is why the crucifix has power. It is why the crescent has power. "In God's name" admits of more than one symbol. It is not the symbol but the *idea symbolized* that makes prayer effective.

Some prayers are more effective than others; some only help us to endure while others transcend conditions and demonstrate an invisible law which has power over the visible. We may consider it a law that insofar as prayer is affirmative it is creative of the desired results.

We are determined to find the secret of this, and it is very simple. The universe is a thing of intelligence projecting itself into experience. Consciousness is impossible unless there is something of which it may be conscious. That of which it is conscious must *take form* that the consciousness may not remain an idle dream.

Following the thought is the thing. Following the prayer is the answer. Following self-knowingness is demonstration. If, then, we are some part of the universal wholeness, does it not follow that "as a man thinketh in his heart, so is he"? This is why the prayer of faith is effective. The affirmative triumphs over the negative, and faith full-orbed steps forth into the power of God.

A treatment is not a petition but an affirmation resting in the belief that it is the nature of Reality to give to us and to express Itself through us. From this sense prayer is an acknowledgment, a statement of acceptance, a belief that the desired thing already is. In such degree as this acknowledgment is complete, petition is transmuted into acceptance, and the mind actually feels that the object of its desire is already an accomplished fact.

Treatment is effective insofar as it agrees with and cooperates with the essential nature of Reality. But those giving the treatment must know that it is a good treatment for it can be no more effective than we know it to be. For instance, if we treat for abundance while at the same time accepting poverty, our words cannot be as effective as they would be should our minds accept plenty; often repeated thoughts, believed in, at last become subjective acceptances, and it is the subjective acceptance which counts. Treatment must convert confusion into peace and thus transcend and transmute the lesser into the greater. Division must pass into unity. The universe withholds no good thing from us, but what belongs to us we must take. In the case of prayer and treatment this taking is a mental act or an act of the mind in acceptance of its natural good.

Any person is good enough to pray or give treatments in an effective manner provided his or her thought keeps in line with the unity of good. Let us learn to feel the indwelling presence of a power which is sufficient to meet all needs; let us learn to accept and to rest in a serene confidence that we have a Divine Partner who is Omnipotent.

If we desire anything, be it money, friendship or what-not, let us turn to the only place we shall ever find Reality—in our own soul as it merges with God. God is already within. If it were not, neither the wit nor the wisdom of humankind could put it there.

There is a creativeness in us which we do not put there, but which we draw out. If we would demonstrate peace and abundance, let us know that this is not done by rushing hither and thither, but by staying at home with the cause. That which the mind recognizes becomes part of its experience. That which we *are* pre-exists our experience. To be still and know that the Eternal Presence is in us is the beginning of wisdom and of freedom.

There is something in us which was never put there by experience but of which all experience is the out-come. Let us consciously enter into the Spirit within, which is, at the same time, both God and humankind. All the good there is, all the power there is, and all the God there is, is the Living Spirit of love and life, the essence of beauty and of truth. The infinite stillness which we drink into the soul is from the great reservoir of the Universe.

Effective treatment convinces the mind that our life is some part of God and that the Spirit is incarnated in us.

Affirmations and denials are for the purpose of convert-
ing thought to a belief in things spiritual. The premise
of correct treatment is perfect God, perfect human and
perfect being. Thought must be reorganized to fit this
premise and must be built on this supposition. We must
believe if we hope to successfully treat; we must have
faith.

If the objection should be raised that having faith calls
for superstition, let us remember this: all the sciences
are built upon faith in principles which experience has
proven to be real. Everything happens as though they
were real and we are justified in believing in them. All
principles are invisible, all laws accepted on faith—there
is no alternative. No one has seen God at any time, nor
has anyone seen goodness, truth or beauty, but who can
doubt their existence? We must learn to have faith.

As practitioners we must have faith in Spirit and complete confidence in our approach to It, must know that
we know and not merely be lukewarm in our convictions. We are to demonstrate that spiritual thought-force
has power over apparent material resistance, and we cannot do this without faith and confidence in our approach
to the principle which we wish to demonstrate.

We must believe in an ever available good and that we
have access to it. We must act as though this good were
real to us; it *must* be real to us if we hope to demonstrate
it. The greatest teacher of applied metaphysics who ever

lived taught the necessity of such faith. Faith has its seed-time and its harvest. Mental treatment repudiates doubt and fear and in their place builds up hope, courage and conviction, expectance and receptivity. The treatment takes place immediately in the thought of the one giving it. Our work begins and ends in our own mind.

It is not our spirit that needs to be made whole; it is our mental reactions to life that need healing. These mental reactions are both conscious and subjective. Successful mental treatment must neutralize negative reactions on both the conscious and the subjective planes. Proper teaching does this for the conscious mind, and proper mental treatment will do it on the subjective side of thought.

Mental healing is accomplished not through a coercion of the consciousness, but through its illumination. We would be neither sick nor unhappy if we were consciously and subjectively unified with good. The practitioner systematically attacks any thought that denies the good of the patient. This is a direct and specific act. And yet the power operative through this act is infinitely greater than the thought of the practitioner. We are using a universal law.

There is a subtle element here—that of knowing the truth and then letting go so that the truth may demonstrate itself. Perhaps this is one of the most difficult things to understand in spiritual work. Our thought is creative, but we do not make it so; it was so before we realized it—not will but willingness; not coercion but conclusion.

We must come to feel that there is a universal goodness, a perfect law and a divine reality flowing through our word. It is impossible to really erase this spiritual conviction. It is implanted by a reality greater than the human mind. There is a power which descends into and operates through the consciousness of the one sensing such power. Real in itself and being ever present, it is as actual as we allow it to become. There is an essence in the invisible world, the emanation of which is the passing of beauty into the form of that which is beautiful, of life into the form of that which lives, the passing of Spirit from an abstract into a concrete state. It is this principle which the practitioner seeks to demonstrate.

Conviction compels the attention of the intellect; it is Reality which floods it. It is the essence of Spirit descending into the intellect, illumining the mind and healing the body. The healing is automatic. The cause is invisible. The effect is tangible and real. The timeless passes into time, the formless into form, the uncreated into that which is created, the prayer into the performance, the treatment into its own demonstration.

The Originating Power descends into the consciousness which meditates upon It and receives It. The intellect abandons itself to the divine ideal. It is a feeling, a sense, an atmosphere. We do not have to energize this power, for it is the very essence of all energy. It is its nature to operate on our word; it will always remain true to its nature. We do not have to wonder whether it will work or is working. It has to work.

The argument of practitioners, if there is an argument, is not whether the power will work, but whether we can mentally rise above any negation that is being experienced to a consciousness of that which is desirable. We must meet the condition as it actually is, in fact, and cause our thoughts to transcend it in every respect. Our argument, then, is between anything which denies good and a sense which we must have that good is, and is the only power. We must know of the availability of this good and believe that it is now responding to us.

Our argument is not with the condition which we wish to see changed, for, of itself, it is neither person, place nor thing. It is a condition and lives merely as a reflection of something behind it. This something is mind at work creating images of self-recognition which are automatically projected into form. There is no mental coercion, nor willpower, no strenuous demand made upon the universe. The demand is made upon ourselves, as the practitioners. The argument takes place within the minds of those giving the treatment and is finished when our minds reach the conclusion that there is nothing but good.

If we seek to combat evil we should be careful that we do not make the evil real. There is a place in the mind which intuitively knows that good overcomes evil, and there is a place which knows no evil to overcome. Our argument, then, is between the experience of evil and a solid conviction that good is the only reality. The law of life cannot produce death. Wholeness cannot will to create apartness. Omniscience cannot will ignorance, and God did not make the devil.

The real person is already free, complete, perfect and in heaven right now. We are already provided with everything necessary to our happiness. How foolish this sounds in light of our experience, and yet this is the right mental attitude to take in giving treatments. This is what confuses so many people. But we are speaking of the real person and not the person of experience. There could be no person of experience unless there were first a real person.

How much life, abundance, goodness, truth and beauty can we mentally entertain—this is the measure of our possible experience; this is the mold of acceptance. The infinite fills all molds and flows forever into new and greater ones. It is the unborn possibility of limitless experience. We give birth to it.

We should be careful not to divide our mental house against itself; having announced the law of liberty, we must not deny it in our experience. Though the whole world has suffered a sense of limitation, there is no limitation to the universe. When all shall know the truth, then the ways, methods and means will be found for the freedom of all people.

The world is slow in waking up to reality, but *we* need not wait. Though the whole world were unhappy, peace still would be. It is our business to demonstrate that harmony is real and discord unreal, that good is real no matter how much evil people may be experiencing. It is on this basis alone that we can use the greatest law of life.

Good never compromises with its opposite. The one practicing must be able to look a fact in the face and say that it is not there. This will not be irrational to the one who has made a careful study of the Science of Mind and Spirit.

Truth knows no opposites. When we take away the belief in evil it flees with the dissolution of this belief. We must be continually reminding ourselves of the power of the word and of our ability to consciously use it. We must know that truth produces freedom because truth is freedom. We are not God, but we are some part of the power of God. It is in quiet expectancy and in calm confidence that our work should be done. The results rest in the eternal law of good.

Helping Others

The idea of helping others through mental treatment should not seem strange; thousands of people have been helped through the *prayers* of others. One of the principal tenets of all religions is that prayer is an actual, intelligent and dynamic force. The chief cornerstone of the present-day Higher-Thought Movement is the fact, already proven in countless thousands of cases, that we *can* help others through mental treatment.

This principle has been so completely proven that millions of people now consider it a positive, definite fact in everyday life. It is no longer a question as to whether we can help others but rather what are the best methods. Must all mental treatment be individual, or is group healing possible? Should the practitioner be with the patient while the treatment is being given, or is the treatment just as effective in the case of physical distance between the two? What is a treatment, and how may we know when we have complied with the law in such a way as to make our mental work effective? These are the questions that people are asking today in order that they may put their faith into actual practice and thus experience in their everyday lives the results of a conscious spiritual endeavor.

Let us then analyze the principle and practice of this work. The principle involved is the underlying mental and spiritual universe in which we live—a universe of positive intelligence governed by absolute law; as there are laws inherent in matter, so there are laws inherent in mind and Spirit. The physical universe is a lower plane than mind or Spirit. This does not mean that human thought creates the world, nor does it mean that human minds control the destinies of the planets; for, according to the law of mind, intelligence can control only what it can grasp.

We are some part of this Universal Wholeness—how much no person has yet been able to fathom—but we are limited by the lack of a clear comprehension of Reality and of our unity with It and the laws governing It and us. Our knowledge of Reality, however, is sufficient to demonstrate new and better experiences. Since we all sense more than we have ever experienced, there must be something within us which is transcendent—a mental and a spiritual principle which rises spontaneously in our thought and which is endowed with capacities that, in our everyday life, we have never fully realized.

It is through the medium of this greater mind, this broader field of spiritual realization, that practitioners work; calling upon the deeper side of life, upon that Universal Medium which unites all people and all events into one unitary wholeness. Therefore, so far as practitioners are concerned, there is no difference between an absent and a present treatment; we need only to know whom we wish to help. Realizing that in the field of Mind and Spirit there is no apartness, we speak the word for the other person in full confidence that the law will operate upon it, but are not concerned where the person is whom we desire to help, or what that person may be doing at that particular time. We are concerned only with our own thoughts relative to that person while endeavoring to bring out in our own minds the realization that this person is a spiritual entity governed by a perfect law, directed by positive intelligence and animated by Divine Life.

Granted that someone asks for help and is receptive to it, why should not the word of practitioners rise through the person's expectation and create in him or her the same degree of realization which the practitioners experience, even though the two may be miles apart? Since the Principle involved is a spiritual unit it must be as conscious of Itself in one as in another, and conscious of Itself at all places simultaneously.

When practitioners have declared that our words are for the person whom we name, we have made the only connection with the patient that is necessary; the rest will depend upon the receptivity of the patient. On the spiritual plane there is no barrier to thought. This does not mean that we are without identity on the subjective plane. Since the Universal Being is perfect, the Spiritual Being of every person is now complete and perfect within Itself and may draw directly upon that Eternal Reservoir of Life in which all live, move and have their being. If the mind were acquainted with this reality, and reflected only harmony and peace, there would be no trouble in the physical world. Where does the treatment, contemplation, meditation, prayer or aspiration for the other person take place? Where could it take place other than in the mind of the one giving the treatment? In other words, if one wishes to help a person who desires to receive such help, the only connection necessary is a definite knowledge on the part of the practitioner for whom and for what the word is intended.

Practitioners think within themselves, about someone;

after definitely stating for whom this word is spoken, we seek to realize the spiritual, mental and physical perfection of this person. We do this in our own minds; and since our minds are functioning in the Universal Mind, in which each individual mind functions, the realization will rise to fulfillment in the one desiring help according to his or her receptivity.

No hypnotism, no mesmerism and no suggestion enters into a scientific mental and spiritual treatment. It is a recognition, on the part of those giving the help, of the perfection of the one wishing to receive this help. Our words are acted upon by a Universal Principle which is ever present and which animates everything; there is a law which operates upon the words. How do we know this? We have never seen this law; neither have we seen the creative law of the soil which operates upon the seed, yet we see the flower and learn by experience that there is such a law. In the same way—through experience—we know there is a law which operates upon the words.

If we wish to help someone who desires help, we speak the patient's name, then, not *willing,* but quietly believing in our own words. We state that this person is a spiritual being—living *now* in a state of harmony—that every thought of doubt, uncertainty and fear is leaving him or her; that this word which we speak, through the great law of harmony, establishes, in him or her, this same recognition. We must be sure to incorporate in each treatment the realization that all people are surrounded by a perfect wisdom which guides them—a universal law of good which protects them. If there is any reason to suppose that they doubt this, we must seek so to form our treatment as to overcome their doubt.

In successful mental treatment the belief which causes the trouble must be changed, and a realization of peace and poise established. There are certain underlying fears which are common to most people—the fear of pain, suffering, poverty, death, of the future and the hereafter, the fear of being misunderstood, and what we might call the fear of the world. These fears practitioners must neutralize, by establishing the consciousness of the one we are helping in the realization that there is nothing to be afraid of, since there is a Universal Intelligence which governs, guides and directs. This Intelligence is Goodness.

The mind must come to sense that life is good, that there is nothing to fear. It must be open to the higher realms of consciousness where the spiritual sun is forever shining. Then automatically the mind will become illumined; it is the mind which governs the lower principles of life. When our minds are governed by the Truth everything which we do will be governed by the Truth, and who is there so far from the nature of Reality as to deny such a Divine government?

So much for personal help, that is, the process of a practitioner working directly for an individual. While it is true that this type of work is always the most effective, it is equally true, and proven by repeated demonstration, that group healing is possible. For instance, at the Institute of Religious Science, in Los Angeles, we have daily healing meditations conducted by groups who are trained in the art of spiritual thinking and whose conviction of the results following this manner of thought is positive.* In the last several years thousands of people have directly benefited through this work, which should not seem strange to us when we realize that one person may stand in front of a microphone and speak to millions of people, provided they are listening. It should not seem unlikely that a group of those believing in the Truth and expecting the Law to work in accordance with their faith should be able to broadcast a meditation which could rise in the consciousness of thousands of people simultaneously—provided they also join in the same spiritual aspiration.

We have proven that thousands of people, some at a great distance and some present in the room, have directly benefited as a result of these meditations—it is the fruits gathered from experience that we are dealing with, rather than a forlorn hope.

---

*United Church of Religious Science, which superseded the Institute of Religious Science, currently provides a similar service. Trained practitioners offer affirmative prayer on a twenty-four-hour basis to anyone who requests it. They may be reached by calling (800) 421-9600 or by writing World Ministry of Prayer, P.O. Box 75127, Los Angeles, CA 90075.

What I Believe

This topic is naturally divided into three parts: what I believe about God, what I believe about humankind, and what I believe about the relationship between God and humankind.

First, I believe that God is Universal Spirit, and by Spirit I mean the Life Essence of all that is—that subtle and intelligent Power which permeates all things and which, in each individual, is conscious mind. I believe that God is Universal Spirit, present in every place, conscious in every part, the Intelligence and mind of all that is.

I believe that humankind is the direct representative of this Divine Presence on this plane of existence. I believe that the relationship between God and the individual is a direct one and that the avenue through which the Spirit expresses Itself to us is through our minds. Our ability to think, to know and to act are direct channels through which the Universal Spirit flows.

It does not seem necessary, to me, that we approach God through any formula or intermediary, but rather that the Spirit of God, the Eternal Mind, is the power by which we think and know. It is self-evident that the only God we can know is the God our consciousness perceives.

But some will say that while it is true that we cannot think outside ourselves, we can know of that which is outside the self. This is true, as is the fact that we have a city hall, but it would have no reality to me unless I was first aware of its existence. This is true of everything, and while the possibility of knowledge may and must expand, we are ignorant of that which we do not perceive.

Therefore, I believe that God is to each one what that person is to God. The Divine Nature must be Infinite, but we know only as much of this Nature as we embody; in no other way can God be known to us. I believe the relationship between God and humankind is hidden within, and when we discover a new truth, or have a better understanding about an old truth, it is really more of this Infinite Mind revealing Itself through us.

I believe in a direct communication between the Spirit

and the individual—the Universal Spirit personifying Itself through each and all; this is a beautiful, a logical, and an unavoidable conclusion. This makes of the human a Divine being, a personification of the Spirit; but if we are Divine Beings why is it that we are so limited and forlorn, so poor, miserable and unhappy? The answer is that we are ignorant of our own nature, and ignorance of the Law excuses no one from its effects.

I believe that all things are governed by immutable and exact laws. These laws cannot be changed nor violated; our ignorance of them will offer no excuse for their infringement, and we are made to suffer, not because God wills it, but because we are ignorant of the truth of our being. We are individuals and have free will and self-choice. We shall learn by experience things mental and physical. There is no other way to learn, and God Himself could not provide any other way without contradicting His own nature. The Spirit is subject to the law of Its own nature, and so are we.

If everything is governed by law, is there any spontaneous mind in the universe? Yes, but this spontaneous Mind never contradicts Its own nature, never infringes Its own law. I believe that everything is governed by exact law; I believe in all scientific truth. But should those in the scientific world, realizing that all is governed by law, thereby exclude a spontaneous Spirit pervading all things, I would ask them this question:

"By what intelligence do you recognize that all things are governed by exact laws?" And they would be compelled to answer, by reason of a spontaneous intelligence welling up within them.

We are living in a mechanical universe governed by laws which have no conscious intelligence or personal volition. But the very fact that we can make this declaration proves that we are not governed by mechanical law alone, for mechanical law cannot, by reason of its very nature, recognize itself. When we come to self-recognition we have already arrived at spontaneous life and self-knowingness.

We are subject to the law of our being, but this law is not one of bondage but one of liberty–liberty under law. I can conceive of a spontaneous Spirit and a retroactive law–and this position has been accepted by deep thinkers of every age. It is self-evident. Since Spirit can never contradict Itself, being pure Intelligence, the life of the Spirit remains harmonious and calm, complete and perfect. Spirit realizes Its nature by personifying Itself, and arrives at self-recognition through what It knows and does.

God operates through what we call the law of evolution or unfoldment, and we are subject to this law. It is not a limitation, but is the way through which freedom and individuality express. There is an unfolding principle within us which is ever carrying us forward to greater and greater expressions of freedom, love, joy and life.

Each one is, I feel, on the pathway of an endless expression of life, truth and beauty. Behind us is the All; before us, within us and expressing through us, is the All. I believe in the immortality and the continuity of the individual stream of consciousness. Humanity is an ascending principle of life, individuality and expression through experience and unfoldment.

I do not believe in hell, devil or damnation, in any future state of punishment, or any of the strange ideas which have been conceived in the minds of morbid people. God does not punish people. There is, however, a Law of Cause and Effect, which governs all and which will automatically punish, impartially and impersonally, if we conflict with its principle of harmony. It is one thing to believe in hell and damnation and quite another proposition to believe in a law of just retribution.

I am sure that full and complete salvation will come at last alike to all. Heaven and hell are states of consciousness in which we now live according to our own state of being. We need worry neither about reward nor punishment, for both are certain. Eventually all will be saved from themselves through their own experiences; this is the only salvation necessary and the only one that could be intelligent.

I believe in every religion that exists, for it is an avenue through which people worship God. I believe in my own religion more than that of anyone else, because this is the avenue through which I worship God.

I do not believe that there is anything in the universe which is against us but ourselves. Everything is and must be for us. The only God who exists, the "Ancient of days," wishes us well, knows us only as being perfect and complete. When we shall learn to know as God knows, we shall be saved from all mistakes and trouble. This is heaven.

The apparent imperfection is but a temporary experience of the soul on the pathway of its unfoldment. It is a creature of time and of the night, but the dawn of an everlasting morning of pure joy is in store for all. Meantime, God is with us and we need have no fear, for "He doeth all things well." We should rejoice in the truth we now have and look toward the future in confident expectancy. As we gain greater understanding we shall receive greater illumination.

I believe that we are surrounded by an intelligent law which receives the impress of our thought and acts upon it. This is the law of our life and we may use it consciously and for definite purposes. I am not superstitious about this law any more than I would be about the law of electricity or any other natural law, for nature is always natural.

I believe in a religion of happiness and joy. There is too much depression and sorrow in the world. These things were never meant to be and have no real place in the world of reality. Religion should be like the morning sun sending forth its rays of light; it should be like the falling dew covering the land with fragrance and sweetness, like the cool of evening and the repose of night. It should be a spontaneous song of joy and not a funeral dirge. From the fullness of a joyous heart the mouth should speak.

I believe in the brotherhood of humanity, the Parenthood of God and a unity binding all together in one perfect whole. I believe the Spirit is in the wind and wave, and manifests Its presence throughout all Nature. But most completely, through our own minds and in our hearts, It proclaims our livingness and Its lovingness.

II

Effective Prayer

Introduction

No longer is there any question or doubt that prayer can change things. There is no aspect of life that it cannot affect. Through prayer, life can become a continuing experience of health, happiness, success, joy and abundance.

Prayer is a very personal thing, a dialogue between a person and his or her Maker. No person can tell another how to pray, any more than another can be told how he or she should always think. However, the question arises as to just what is involved in making prayer effective in a controlled manner.

It appears that there are certain requisites which are the

basis for effective prayer. First of all, prayer has its foundation in one's religious beliefs. Certain religious convictions seem to be detrimental to prayers being answered, while others provide a basis for outstanding results.

The first part of this section presents ideas on how to use the power of prayer. At heart, Dr. Holmes was a great teacher, and here he guides the reader into understanding the nature of prayer and how to use it in an effective manner.

In the second part will be found a variety of practical suggestions for effective prayer, or spiritual mind treatment as Dr. Holmes termed it. The ideas brought forth here are aids which will enable the individual to have his or her prayers be more specific factors in life. These are ideas which he presented in instructing a special class in creative prayer, and they are presented in what might be termed outline form.

Throughout the ages prayer has been an important factor in human life. Regardless of different religious convictions or cultural backgrounds prayer has been found to be productive of results.

This would imply that there is some universal factor involved, although it has been interpreted in many ways. For prayer to consistently have the desired result seems to depend upon going behind the various interpretations, the superstitions involved, the dogma and ritual, and getting back to the basic factor itself.

To do this requires a certain degree of understanding of the nature of Life and humankind, an understanding that is based on the spiritual wisdom of the ages and at the same time incorporates the truth of the ever-advancing front of knowledge in today's world.

The Practice

To use prayer in a practical and effective manner certain things must be considered as necessary.

Some may believe that prayer must follow a formula, a certain ritual, which may be adequate for them. It has been found that for greater efficacy prayer needs to have more freedom of expression, a greater flexibility. For this reason it is felt that instead of prayer being a formula, there is a basic technique which may be followed by the individual and adapted to his or her own particular personality and need.

Here are presented ideas which have proved to be valid by all who have used them. People of all religious denominations have applied them in their prayer life and have discovered an entire new world of living open up.

What the great, the good, and the wise of all ages
have taught, which is also the very foundation of modern psychology and science, is that the universe is a
spiritual system. This does not deny the physical universe, which is a part of it.

So when we say that our body is a spiritual body we
are not saying that we have no eyes, or we have no feet,
or we have no stomach. These things are all included in
the spiritual system. God's world is not a world of illu-
sions but of realities. The illusion is not in the thing but
in the way we look at it and think about it. Everything
is as real as it is supposed to be.

We live in the physical universe, the nature of which
appears to be, first of all, as though there were a Divine
Presence, a universal Spirit, an infinite Person back of it.
God as pure Spirit, as infinite Person, also is always per-
sonal to each one of us, always personified in us. The
God that is everywhere is also in us.

There could be only goodness in the nature of God,
or God would be self-destructive. Plato said that God is
goodness, truth and beauty. A modern prophet said that
God is life, truth and love. They are both correct. God
is the Essence of life, the Essence of intelligence, the
Divine Presence everywhere present, and therefore at
the center of our own being.

We are more than a reflection of God, more than an
emanation or a projection of God; we are an attribute,

an incarnation, an individualization. There is nothing else we could be. Naturally, as a result there is a pressure against us at all times to be like God: lovable, beautiful, joyous, whole, complete, satisfied.

We are not only surrounded by the Divine Presence, we are also immersed in the infinite Law, which has no warmth, no color. It is not a person; It is a Principle responding to us creatively by corresponding with our mental attitudes. We differentiate between God as the infinite Person, the Divine Presence, and the Law as the Divine Principle. One is the engineer and the other the engine.

There must be both, otherwise we could not have a complete cosmology or a complete philosophy of life. That God is infinite Person and is at the same time infinite Law is what physicist Sir James Jeans meant when he said that we can think of the universe as an infinite Thinker thinking mathematically. The infinite Thinker is the Person, and thought is manifested through the Law of Its own nature. Everywhere we look we see that the universe is a combination of the Presence and the Law.

Certain fundamental principles do exist in the physical universe, and they operate mechanically and mathematically. Similarly, we find that we are surrounded by and immersed in a Law of Mind, a creative medium which automatically acts upon or reacts to our every thought. People like Emerson, known as one of the ten greatest intellects who ever lived, thought, and rightly we may be sure, that for every law of nature that we observe—such as those in chemistry and physics—we shall some day find a corresponding spiritual or mental law. That is why Emerson said that he believed in a law of parallels. This would mean that for every law that science discovers we will find a comparable spiritual one. This is why Dr. Alexis Carrel said that faith, without violating any physical law, uses another set of laws that transcend physical laws.

The Bible says: "And the earth was without form, and void; and darkness was upon the face of the deep. And the Spirit of God moved upon the face of the waters." All creation is the result of Divine Ideas going forth through Law into manifestation.

These ideas are the essence of what the great of the ages have always taught. It is all very simple, but one of our great troubles is that we mentally get uneasy when we think we are going to have to think. But thinking is the easiest thing in the world; however, we need to do it in a constructive manner.

We can interpret the teaching of Jesus as being built on the assumption, the theory, that there is *something* that reacts to our thought exactly as we think it. This is what creation is. The Word of God manifested in definite form. That which is created is not a cause, but it is an effect. We are one with the Creator and that which is created. We are in it, with it, like it, a part of it. We did not make it that way and we cannot change it. There is nothing we can do about it other than to accept it and utilize our position in it.

How shall we do this? How do we use any law? We use the laws of electricity consciously, simply, directly and by personal choice. The laws of electricity have no volition. So it is with the use of the Law of Mind. We must use It with full awareness. But we must remember that the Law of Mind, or Spirit, which we may use consciously, will always return to us exactly what we are thinking. We cannot conceal anything. The Bible says: ". . . there is nothing covered, that shall not be revealed; and hid, that shall not be known." Shakespeare said: "This above all: to thine own self be true. And it must follow, as the night the day, Thou canst not then be false to any man." Emerson said: "What you are stands over you the while, and thunders so that I cannot hear what you say to the contrary."

We need to be fully aware that we cannot fool the Law of Cause and Effect, that thought becomes manifested. We can fool each other, and unfortunately we fool ourselves most of the time, but the Law of Mind is as a law of reflection returning to us the exact content of our thought.

This Law is not a physical law as such. It is comparable to the laws of science but applies to the realm of

Mind and Spirit. It is a Law which responds to our word; that is, our thought, mental image or idea. Everything that is must first exist in the Mind of God, or our mind, as an idea which is then projected into form.

In our lives we may find comparable situations in psychosomatic medicine, which seeks to uncover mental causes for physical ailments. It finds patterns of thoughts, collections or clusters of thoughts, which are producing physical correspondents. Emotional strain and stress has been found to cause great physical repercussions. There is an invisible but adequate cause for every condition that exists in our lives.

We have much in our lives that we do not enjoy and that we would like to get rid of. There is nothing wrong about using the Law of Mind for any good we desire providing it does not interfere with another person's good. We should always ask ourselves if what we wish produces harmony, and then be sure there is no hurt in it to anyone.

We can only come into the experience of harmony by thinking harmoniously. So no matter what we profess, what the lips say, it is only from the mind and heart that the experiences of life come. So to begin to constructively use the Law of Mind rests on the conversion of our consciousness. Our life on the outer is a reflection of the inner.

If God is in every place there can be no place where God is not. So in the midst of the storm there is a calm; in the center of every person's life is pure Spirit. But we can get back to It only by imbibing the nature of Its Being and the spirit of Its Nature; that is, by being like It. So we must change our thought patterns.

The creative nature of our thought involves the sum total of the content of our mind. This means that our habitual thought patterns are being reflected in all our images of thought. Also, the subconscious mind is a great creative reservoir. Then, we are all immersed in and experiencing the race consciousness, and it is operating through each one of us to a greater or lesser degree. Any negativity of thought we are aware of arising from such sources may be changed by consciously identifying ourselves with and maintaining only good, positive ideas. Such new identification thus becomes the law of our life.

If everything there is is the operation of Intelligence on or through Law, the Word of God upon the waters, then our every word is an idea which automatically has the seed of fulfillment in it. The idea is the seed that takes root in the Law of Mind, which in turn produces the results. Moses said: ". . . the word is . . . in thy mouth. . . ." Every word you speak, every idea, whether positive or negative, is a creative factor. ". . . the Word was made flesh, and dwelt among us. . . ."

We do not change Reality. But our thoughts are like writings on a blackboard; they may be rubbed out and replaced by others. We must not only continuously identify ourselves with the desires of our heart, being certain they do not deny goodness, but must erase and remove all contrary ideas. Jesus indicated that God desires us to have every good thing. The song of a joyous life is always being sung, but we do not hear it. But God cannot give us love through hate; God cannot give us peace through confusion; God cannot give us happiness through misery; God cannot give us joy through our tears. God cannot express harmony through discord. God cannot express in opposites. If He did He would destroy Himself, which He cannot do. Because of this Jesus said: "Ye cannot serve God and mammon." And in the Bhagavad Gita we find the admonition that we will have to do away with the pairs of opposites. We cannot walk east and west at the same time.

We have to learn that if we want to draw out of the Divine Nature that which is in It, we must cooperate with the nature of Its Being. That is the only limitation that is set on humankind. What we may believe about It will not change It. All the belief the world has ever had about hell never created any hell outside of the discord in the consciousness of the people who believed in it. There is no more chance that there is a hell than there is in the idea that God is the devil.

To experience goodness we will have to identify ourselves with goodness. That is not easy. For instance, we start the day by saying, "I am going to believe only in harmony." Then we see a headline in the paper, we listen to the radio and talk with each other. Then we say, "Well, harmony is in God—in heaven. I wish it were here on earth." In this way we separate ourselves from it. We should not only refuse to comment on the discord, but we should not even dare to hold it in our thought. To think about a thing is to will to do it, and to have the will to do it is to bring it about in our lives.

We will have to learn to think straight. What does this mean in actual practice? For example, we will take the case of a person who thinks he or she has no friends. Loneliness is one of the greatest diseases in the world, a sense of aloneness, of not belonging to the universe, a sense that no one cares. More people suffer from this than from anything else, and it produces a larger percentage of suffering than all other diseases. We should instruct such a person to realize that:

"God is in you. God is in everyone else. There is One Mind common to all individuals. There is One Person. All people are in this One Person; every person is a personification of this One; therefore there is something in you that is one with every other person you will ever meet. Solve your problem by never again believing anything else. Identify yourself with that One in everyone you meet; know that everyone you meet is just a little different expression of that One, and meet them as that One, and you will meet yourself in that One."

Everything is good up to now, very easy to understand, but what the patient is called on to do is hard. Perhaps the first time he or she goes out someone will say something unkind to this person, who will say, "I don't see the One in that one." We should not condemn, but sympathize, because we are talking about ourselves. We only react to our own reactions. This person is hurt, feels badly inside. What is he or she going to do? Start all over again. Gradually the word which the patient affirms will happen to him or her through the action of the Law of Mind—a Law of Cause and Effect.

The subjective content of our mind is very much greater than we are consciously aware of. Not only is it our silent power of attraction and repulsion, but it represents the true polarity of the mind. However, there is nothing in it that was not put there, and what we put into it we can take out. But there must be a conversion, a catharsis, a purging of the negative subjective emotional content of our thought. Gradually, by identifying ourselves with love, happiness, friendship and harmony, our thought patterns change, and then we will encounter only situations which are like them, no matter where we go or whom we may meet. Emerson announced this when he said: "The only way to have a friend is to be one." Love everybody! We cannot afford the self-imposed ravages of hate.

Remember we are always working with an immutable Law, an unfailing Principle, an available Power. Those who do this will see the day when the desires of their hearts will become the facts of their experience. This can be accomplished with any aspect of life, no matter what it is—love, success or health.

The Law of Mind works as a law of identity, reproducing identically the content of our thought in and as our experience. It works by involution and evolution. We must get the ideas into the mind and allow them to work out. But very frequently people do not realize this and do not give the Law a chance to work. It is like planting seeds in the garden and then tearing them out again before they come to fruition. We must watch the seeds of thought and cultivate them. We must separate the ideas with intelligence, separating the wheat from the chaff and saving the wheat. God always gives the increase if we trust in and rightly use the Law of God's nature.

It is as simple as this: We are surrounded by an infinite Law that can do anything. There is no limit to It and It does not know anything about big and little. But what the Law does for us It must do through us. Therefore our problem is to convert our own thought. We must consciously and subjectively accept only that which we wish to experience.

We convert the mind by the audible or silent expression and acceptance of constructive words, thoughts, ideas or beliefs. This is prayer, communion, realization or meditation—whatever we choose to call it. Thus we automatically change our thought patterns through the Law of Cause and Effect. As our thinking rises to a higher comprehension of the nature of Spirit—the Source of health, beauty, love, life and abundance—automatically our thought patterns are improved and become more productive of good in our lives.

We must imbibe and embody a sense of both the Divine Presence and the infinite Law. As we do so we may with surety affirm that our thoughts and ideas become more Divine-like in their nature. We need to be more concerned about getting our thought straightened out than about the results that will follow, for they will follow automatically as night the day.

For clearer thinking in what we call a spiritual mind treatment, effective prayer, we watch ourselves, and see if in it we have placed any limitation relative to the past, present or future which may limit the possibility of its complete fulfillment. If we have, we are automatically causing the Law to act through that limitation and not to act freely on the good that is desired. We are conditioning the action of the Law to what we have accepted—good or bad. Jesus stated the whole thing simply when he said: ". . . as thou hast believed, so be it done unto thee. . . ."

We must watch over our own thought carefully, painstakingly, patiently, and not become discouraged. Just as surely as we do this we are bound to have our prayers become effective in our experience. The one who successfully uses spiritual mind treatment is merely one who knows these things, practices them, and understands and believes them. Through experience one learns that when one does this the result will be certain for any person, situation or condition. The Spirit responds alike to everyone.

We may control our thinking, and this can be done if we will but do it. It does not matter what someone else thinks. The only thing that matters is this: that in the integrity of our own soul, the union of our own consciousness with God and the Universe, that thing which we demand of the Spirit within will happen, that good which we accept as ours will come to pass. And finally, sooner or later, all people who are awake and alive will know themselves. They will come to self-awareness, and that self-awareness will include a knowledge of their union with Life. They will become whole within themselves. What a wonderful thing to contemplate!

We must always realize that we are in conscious partnership, now, with the Infinite, and the good word that goes forth from our mouth, even as the word of Jesus, is the Word of God. Then as that word demonstrates itself in our individual lives, everyone we meet whom we can help will ask for that help, and we shall have demonstrated that which all the ages have passionately looked forward to.

Practical
Suggestions

Everyone desires that his or her prayers be effective. Probably the most valuable aid today in this respect is the teaching and philosophy advanced by Science of Mind.

The following pages contain aids, suggestions and vital ideas which relate to prayer for specific purposes. They can help you clarify your thinking so that it can be more creative and constructive.

However, they need to be interpreted in your own way, they need to be made yours, for only then do they add vitality to your prayers.

Effective prayer is both an art and a science, a thing of the heart and the intellect. With these ideas you can come to develop your prayer life to a point where it is a continuously creative factor for your daily joy of living.

It is certain that none of you receive as much benefit from your prayers or spiritual mind treatments as you might. You do not permit your consciousness to range in the field of greater possibilities. A certain time should be taken definitely each day for the enlargement of consciousness. This is done by reminding your imagination that the field with which it deals is limitless; that Mind is the creator and the sustainer; that Mind is infinite, ever available and always responsive to you.

The basic principle upon which spiritual mind treatment rests is that there is creative power in thought; that Truth known is demonstrated, and that right ideas are manifested by the Law of Mind. The power to act resides in Spirit. The action of Spirit is the movement of consciousness. Your understanding of this, your comprehension of spiritual Power, enables you to use the Law of Mind for specific purposes.

God manifests through us in our ideas. The idea is correct when you have a spiritual sense of it, when you substitute a consciousness of unity for a consciousness of separation. In other words, you are using the Principle correctly when you substitute spiritual ideas for objective facts and proceed upon the basis that new ideas create new facts.

Through the process of thought you may remove old and undesirable ideas, replacing them with new and more constructive ones which can then become a definite program for right action for you. The process of knowing that this is happening and declaring that right ideas are made known to you constitutes an important step in spiritual mind treatment.

You should forever increase this receptivity, continuously extend and expand your comprehension. You should declare a hundred times a day: "Good and more good is mine. An ever-increasing good is mine. There is no limit to the good which is mine. Everywhere I go I see this good, I feel it, I experience it. It presses itself against me, flows through me, expresses itself in me and multiplies itself around me."

Your consciousness of good is acted upon by the Law of Mind. Such awareness acts as a law of elimination and expulsion to every discord, to every sense of accumulated bondage, to every sense of impure congestion or accumulation. Your prayer directs the Law and is the motivation of Its power. Be sure you do not deny your own understanding.

The inertia of human thought, rising as it does from the morbidity of race consciousness and the mesmeric grip of race suggestion, seeks to claim that there is not in or through you the power to heal. Recognize this false argument for what it actually is. It is nothing claiming to be something. It is a lie claiming to be the truth. It is a habit of thought unwilling to surrender itself.

You must know that your prayer absolutely dispels

and obliterates and shakes loose this mental inertia, and frees the consciousness to right action. Any and all sense of discord is but false conclusion about the truth.

You must increasingly come to understand that you have access to the infinite creative power of Law, and you must always be aware that in the infinite Presence rests the universal Principle of Perfection. Not only in every way reaffirming Its Presence, you must in every possible way establish within your own consciousness a feeling for It, a sense about It.

Heal the discordant thought and the Principle of Perfection, which always pervades your path, will establish harmony in your experience. Know that It does this immediately, that there is no process of time. Every spiritual mind treatment must incorporate within it the consciousness of completion, of perfection, of fulfillment, in the here and in the now.

There should never be any sense of finality in your self-discovery. No matter how much good you experience today, you should expect more tomorrow. Expectancy always speeds progress; anticipation of better-yet-to-come helps to dissolve the load of disbelief which you now carry with you. You must learn to free your consciousness. Nothing is too good to be true. Harmony is already an ever-present Reality, but as far as you are concerned, It waits to be perceived and only as much good can come to you as you mentally accept.

*   *   *   *

The denials used in treatment are for the purpose of removing from consciousness any belief which accepts the idea that there is any manifestation of perfect Spirit which need be diseased. There is neither origin nor cause for disease in pure Spirit. Disease, of itself, is a very factual thing, but not a thing Divinely ordained.

To affirm that the Perfection of God is manifested in you and to deny the negative fact does not mean that you are practicing duality, but that you are coming into a complete comprehension of your unity with God. Very frequently denials are necessary in spiritual mind treatment, and you should not hesitate to use them whenever they are necessary.

You must never overlook the fact that spiritual mind treatment is not only a thing of consciousness, but that it is an *active state* of consciousness. It contains definite statements. The treatment moves to a definite end, a specific conclusion that God is all there is and that His Perfection is now manifested. But if, in its process, it is necessary to mentally remove obstructions, then the denial does this.

There is but One Healer. This is the Spirit–God. There is but One Life Principle. This is the action of God in us. There is but One final Law. This is the Law of Mind. There is but One ultimate Impulsion. This Impulsion is Love.

When you array your ideas of the nature of God against the evidence of appearances, you should be certain that the conclusions you reach are positive ones and outweigh all negative ideas which would contradict them. The effectiveness of your treatment lies entirely in your state of consciousness, in whether or not you really are able to perceive more good than evil in any condition or situation.

You should have a calm which transcends the distorted thought and confusion about any condition. You should have a sense of eternal justice which outweighs any belief in, or manifestation of, temporary injustice, and a sense of abundance which completely transmutes a lesser concept of bondage into one of liberty.

It is not enough merely to state your belief or to affirm it as a conviction—this is but the foundation upon which you build your edifice of faith. These are the materials which you mold into the form of definite desire. You must not only know that God is all there is, but you must know that God exists right where the need is—not in the form of the need, but in the form of the answer to the need. The Divine Spirit is the only Actor, the All-in-All, and is now manifesting Itself. Being All-in-All, It has no opposition, competition or otherness. Firmly being aware of your Oneness with God constitutes a right start in giving a spiritual mind treatment.

In a certain sense it might be said that a treatment is good when you *know* that it is good. In a very definite sense you can have nothing good come out of a treatment unless you first put it into it. From this viewpoint treatment is not a thing of concentration, but is a conscious action. It definitely separates negative thought from positive thought. In an effective treatment you know that there is but One Mind, that this Mind is God, this Mind is good, this Mind is perfect. All movement takes place in this Mind; all action proceeds from this Mind; nothing moves unless Mind moves it.

The creative action of the Mind of God also resides in the human mind. There is One Mind used by you and all of us. All have complete access to this Mind, and you are ever manifesting It at the level of your own comprehension or your own interior awareness of Life. That any disease, discord or negation appears to move in or out of a situation is because your mind first conceives such motion. The treatment must have the conviction that it can move it out rather than in.

All the good there is is available to you, not *some* part of it, but *all* of it. It is not only available, it is usable. It is ever-present and inexhaustible. First know that God is all there is, and that God is available. Then that the Divine Law always responds, and that your treatment causes It to respond in such a way as to remove any negative situation and in its place restore harmony.

Your concept of the Perfection of God as being now manifested in your experience is a spiritual power which heals. Treatment is the activity of right ideas asserting themselves through Law. Your constructive use of the Law of Mind, being on a higher plane of consciousness than the state of thought which produced any discord, must therefore erase it, and you must know that it will do so.

*   *   *   *

The establishment of your good is brought about through the Law of Mind by the power of your own Divinity. Power exists, and the action of this Power is upon your word, or your word acts upon the Power, no one knows which. For all practical intents and purposes, the Power acts upon your word—your spiritual mind treatment—and you establish the word in your own consciousness, with no attempt whatsoever to send it out anywhere.

Never overlook the fact that it is an active consciousness which demonstrates spiritual understanding. While there must be no personal sense of responsibility in healing, you must certainly use your consciousness in such an active way that definite healing may result. To your understanding of the Truth and to your consciousness of Good, you must add an activity of thought. That is, the Law undirected will do nothing,

but directed It can do anything and all things. Therefore, in your treatment you give conscious direction to
the Law.

There is no way of distributing an undistributed
power without first providing a definite channel through
which it may flow. There is no possible way of giving an
effective prayer unless you direct spiritual Power. This is
done definitely as you consciously give direction in
your treatment. It is certain that there must be a definite
receptivity in your thought if any good results are to follow. Too often people overlook this and merely make
abstract statements and so never bring them down to
earth.

In such degree as any person can accept harmony
instead of discord, he or she will demonstrate that harmony without having to create it. Never forget that
while you can *believe* in that which is not so, you can
only *know* that which is really so. Belief that is confused
will produce discord, but belief that is centered on a
concept of harmony will invariably heal discord. There
must be no sense of doubt in your treatment. Treatment
should always be calm, poised, definite and active.

No matter how seemingly impossible any situation
may be, or how difficult the appearance of any problem
may appear, you must never become discouraged. You
must continue to do your work knowing full well that
you are dealing with the invisible Divine Presence and

Principle—the great Reality back of everything.

It would be impossible for you to do this unless you are firmly convinced that Mind is the only creative agency in the universe and that you have direct and conscious access to Its creativity. Moreover, you must be conscious that through right thought and true statements you are making constructive use of the Law of Mind.

Humankind's thought *is* the activity of Mind, for Mind without thought or directed consciousness would have no real existence. There can be no existence apart from consciousness, or if there be any existence apart from consciousness then there is no one, no thing and no intelligence to be aware of such existence. It is evident that without self-awareness there is not only no realization of life, but no life to be realized.

Hence, again you must affirm that Mind in action is Its own Law of fulfillment. When you understand this you will not become discouraged. You will know that if you persist in declaring the truth, the pathway to Reality will be cleared, obstructions will be removed, wrong conditions will be resolved. It follows that you will be happy because you are sure; doubts no longer assail you, fear does not possess you, negation no longer obsesses your thought, and you continue to make your declarations with calm confidence and with Divine assurance.

*   *   *   *

You must be careful never to despise your body, certainly never to deny its reality or the reality of any of its
organs or functions. There is nothing wrong with the
sum total of spiritual Right Ideas that make up your
body. Every organ and every function of the human
body has a Universal Prototype behind it. They are
Ideas in the Mind of God, and perfect Ideas.

You must understand the harmonious arrangement of
these Ideas, the unified and harmonious action between
them. Your word affirms that the spiritual Idea is now
manifested in the flesh—in every organ and function.
Most certainly, you never deny that there is a body; you
merely affirm that the body is a spiritual Idea right now.

To dwell morbidly on any organ or function of the
body is to condemn it, to retard its action, to congest its
movement, to impede the circulation through it, and,
of course, wherever the circulation is impeded the
elimination is also impaired. Every sense of condemnation should be replaced with a sense of praise. You
must know that Divine Action is establishing proper
circulation, perfect assimilation and right elimination.

Nothing can adhere to a spiritual Idea except
freedom, perfection and peace, for God is All-in-All,
over all and through all, and in every organ. The functions of the body are not separate from God, but are

within God. Learn to love all of these functions as being attributes of Spirit and to sense the Divine Universal Harmony underlying all.

The sense of disease and discord is largely in subconscious thought, through which avenue it is transmitted from one person to another or lodged in the general race belief. From this source, through suggestion, it insinuates itself into the consciousness of the individual.

In this way we are all more or less hypnotized from the cradle to the grave, and it is your purpose to free your thought from the bondage of race suggestion. In this case, then, you deal not with disease as a thing in itself, but merely as an experience. It does not belong to you, it is only operating on you.

In your treatment you declare that there is no suggestion, no race belief in this disease which can operate through you, that your spiritual self is perfect, complete, and now dominates your entire being, and that every evidence of discord, fear, doubt or anxiety is eliminated through the power of your word.

This idea in treatment will have as much power as you *know* it will have. The very fact that the whole performance is mental makes this self-evident. For once you assume that there is such a thing as an effective spiritual mind treatment, that assumption also implies that if the treatment is to be effective nothing can come out of it that is not first put into it since it is a thing of thought.

Really, a treatment is a spiritual entity in which is involved the idea that is to evolve and become a part of your experience. Loose it, let it go and then have no doubt but that what is *involved* will *evolve.*

* * * *

In using spiritual mind treatment for a physical healing of others you must be very careful never to condemn the patients from the standpoint of medicine. From the medical viewpoint, people may have physical suffering because of certain antecedent physical conditions. Or the cause may be a heart condition, hypertension, or continuous or excessive mental strain or anxiety. Or they may have the same trouble as a result of over-indulgence, which, according to certain religious beliefs, has been classified as "sin." Or, from the standpoint of a metaphysician, they may have the same trouble as a result of some kind of continued wrong thinking.

Whatever the actual situation may be, you must be very careful that you do not attach the disease to the patients. It would be just as wrong to attach it by saying they have thought wrongly as by saying they have acted wrongly, because you must rise not only above wrong physical reactions, but above wrong mental reactions. To say that people must suffer because of their sins or mistakes is no different from saying they must suffer because they strained themselves physically, and it is only when the depressing fact of such condemnation is removed that a heart could regain and retain its normal action.

This is something which you must be very careful to watch in all of your prayer work. You must rise above both mistake and consequence to the realm of pure Spirit where there was no mistake, hence no negative consequence. Wholeness has never ceased to be exactly what It is. This is the central realization around which your thought should revolve. There is no place for condemnation in your mind when giving a spiritual mind treatment. Nor should you ever feel that you failed to get good results because of the mistakes which your patients persist in repeating. Your business is to clear up your own thought about the patients and leave them in the hands of that Power which is already Perfect.

*   *   *   *

It is entirely possible for all of us, through thought, to condemn the food we eat to such a degree that no matter what we take into our systems it will disagree with us. In this way, people actually poison their food through condemnation. While there is no question that it is a good thing for people to follow a scientific and sensible diet, we must be very careful in so doing that we do not think too much about the food which we are eating.

In most instances it is fear of food and not the food itself which has a bad effect. Hence you must make a complete mental agreement with it, actually love it for the good it can do you, and never eat unless you are in a peaceful, happy frame of mind. It is a well-known fact that when food is taken into the system while one is agitated or mentally upset, the conditions are such that it will neither digest nor eliminate properly. The whole nervous system is thrown out of gear, a sort of strangulation takes place and the digestive process is impeded. All of which can be cleared up by creating the proper mental attitude.

You should think of food as a spiritual Idea, and realize that spiritual Ideas agree with each other in the one Body of Perfection. They are taken in intelligently, assimilated intelligently and eliminated intelligently. Every process is already designed by nature to be perfect, and you must know that there is nothing in you or in the one whom you are seeking to help which can contradict this perfection.

A good treatment for any kind of physical problem is to declare that all things are now perfect, Life is *already* perfect. Your treatment is the acceptance of this right action of Life. It is this acceptance which enables the healing to take place.

The creative word of good which you use is the Word of God in you, manifesting Divine Power, infinite

Wisdom and perfect Action. Spirit, then, is the Principle of Perfection, Harmony and Right Action in every aspect of your body. Your word is the cause of elimination, of expulsion to every improper condition. You know that every thought and belief and appearance of the undesired condition is removed. Your word is the enactment of the Law, the activity of the Spirit, the movement of Divine Power through your body.

In your treatment you naturally start with the supposition that Spirit is the only Life, and that this Life is your life. This Perfect Life is your life now. The Law of Mind establishes your recognition of this Perfection as being your immediate experience. All the Power there is is the Power of the Law of Mind—the creativity of Spirit. The only action there is is the action of Mind or Spirit. Hence, in your word rests the ability to remove anything and everything which does not belong to pure Spirit.

You must believe this and definitely state it. Your statements must be specific, and you must be conscious of their meaning. Without these two elements of thought, treatment cannot be effective.

*   *   *   *

Lack of abundance is not part of the heavenly kingdom. It would be a contradiction of the Divine Nature to think of God as being impoverished. But humankind is impoverished because we do not see the abundance around us. We do not interpret the universe as a spiritual system; we do not recognize the Spirit as the limitless Source back of all supply.

In declaring that the Spirit is the Source of supply you state an eternal verity. But you must follow this declaration with another declaration that this Source *is now your supply*. The idea you use in your treatment is that Spirit manifests as your supply according to your concept of it. You make the specific statement that you are rightly guided and Divinely protected. You know that every good thing is attracted to you, and that everything that makes life full and complete is now manifest in what you are doing, where you are right now, at this present time, today.

Statements similar to this cause the One Source of Supply to take definite form, and the element of time necessary to produce this form is also a thing of consciousness. For there certainly is neither time nor space without awareness. The action of your treatment is in what you call the present time—it is always "today." Hence, the fulfillment and the completion of life is today. The opportunity is today. The door is open now. The chance for complete self-expression is this moment. This concept is basic in all effective treatment.

*   *   *   *

Fear and faith are identical in that the energy used in the one is the same energy used in the other, since there is but one final Energy in the universe and this final Energy is the energy of thought. Fear is a positive acceptance that you shall experience that which you dislike. Faith is a positive acceptance that you shall experience that which you do like. But they are identical in their mental action. The only difference is in the direction.

You should be careful not to fight fear too much, but rather, through a sort of flexible imagination, convert fear into faith. Realizing that it is a mental attitude, you can do this very easily. Looking at the thing which you fear and examining the thought of fear which you have about it, convert this thought into one of faith, realizing that the energy of fear converted into faith will produce an effect exactly opposite.

If you will look at the thing you are afraid of until you really understand it, it will no longer have any element of fear for you. You can do this in such degree as you are conscious of being Divinely guided and protected, and state your realization of this in a definite manner.

Love overcomes both hate and fear. However, love does not overcome hate and fear through controversy, argument or force, but by a subtle power of transformation, transmutation and sublimation. It is invisible in its essence but apparent through its act. As light overcomes the darkness, as the presence of heat causes the coolness of a room to change until it is warm and comfortable, so the radiant action of love and peace dissipates fear, hate and confusion.

Love is the victor in every case. Love breaks down the iron bars of thought, shatters the walls of material belief, severs the chain of bondage which thought has imposed, and sets the captive free.

In treatment you should know that love rules your thought and actions, and that you are appreciated by everyone who contacts you. You affirm that fear and hate cannot motivate you, cannot operate through you, cannot do anything to you, do not belong to you, and are no part of you. Allow nothing to enter your consciousness but a sense of peace.

In effective prayer you know that there is no place for anything but good in your life. You know that you do not contradict what you have affirmed, that the statements you have made are the Truth about you, and that they absolutely, positively, immediately and permanently uproot, cast out and forever obliterate every negative condition or situation to which they are directed. You never let yourself be misled by appearances or limited by the thinking of others. You accept for yourself only those ideas which you intuitively recognize as being Divine in their source.

INDEX

ABOUT THE AUTHOR

Ernest Holmes (1887-1960) was the founder of the Science of Mind philosophy and movement. Ernest Holmes's teachings are based on both Eastern and Western traditions, and the empirical laws of science and metaphysics. Science of Mind is a spiritual philosophy that people throughout the world have come to know as a positive, supportive approach to life. These ancient truths have kept pace with and proven their relevancy in today's global village and its expanding technology and warp-speed changes.

Author of *The Science of Mind*, the seminal book on his teachings, Holmes also founded the monthly periodical, *Science of Mind* magazine, which has been in continuous monthly publication since 1927.

Through lectures, radio, television programs, tape recordings, books and magazines, Ernest Holmes has introduced millions of people to the simple principles of successful living that he called "the Science of Mind." His other works include *Creative Mind, This Thing Called You, How to Change Your Life, Words That Heal Today, La Ciencia de la Mente, Thoughts Are Things* and *This Thing Called Life.*

Also By Ernest Holmes . . .

Thoughts Are Things
Discover the life-changing power of thinking in creative and self-affirming ways.

Code #7214 Quality Paperback • $10.95

Words That Heal Today
Learn the message of your divine heritage by applying the teachings of Jesus and the Apostle Paul to contemporary life.

Code #6854 Quality Paperback • $10.95

How to Change Your Life
This book presents ideas on life and God essential to contemporary spiritual understanding; learn how science and spirituality have merged and what this means to you.

Code #6862 Quality Paperback • $10.95

A New Season of
Chicken Soup for the Soul

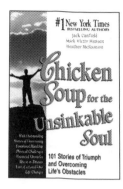
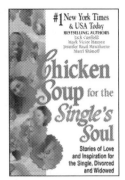

THOUGHTS TO LIVE BY

The graceful, remarkable words in this inspiring collection are filled with purity and love. In our fast-paced world, filled with turmoil and tragedy, the simple and gentle wisdom of the *Kiss of God* is sure to make it a treasured favorite.

Code #7435 Quality Paperback • $9.95

A unique gem of a book, overflowing with profound truths that will help you find meaning and understanding in a sometimes difficult world.

Pearls of Wisdom will guide you to live each day with an open heart.

Code #7230 Quality Paperback • $6.95